Red Tail Captured, Red Tail Free

Memoirs of a Tuskegee Airman and POW

Red Tail Captured,

Alexander Jefferson

LIEUTENANT COLONEL, USAF, RET.

with Lewis H. Carlson

Red Tail Free

FORDHAM UNIVERSITY PRESS   New York 2005

Library of Congress Cataloging-in-Publication Data

Jefferson, Alexander, 1921–
    Red Tail captured, Red Tail free : memoirs of a Tuskegee airman
and POW / Alexander Jefferson, with Lewis H. Carlson.— 1st ed.
      p. cm. — (World War II—the global, human, and ethical
dimension ; no. 5)
    Includes bibliographical references and index.
     1. Jefferson, Alexander, 1921– 2. World War,
1939–1945—Prisoners and prisons, German. 3. World War,
1939–1945—Participation, African American. 4. United States.
Army Air Forces. Fighter Group, 332nd. 5. World War,
1939–1945—Aerial operations, American. 6. World War,
1939–1945—Personal narratives, American. 7. Prisoners of
war—United States—Biography. 8. Prisoners of war—
Germany—Biography. 9. Fighter pilots—United States—
Biography. 10. African American air pilots—Biography.
I. Carlson, Lewis H. II. Title. III. World War II—the global
human, and ethical dimention ; 5.
  d806.G3J43 2005
  940.54'4973'092—dc22

                                       2004029414

Printed in the United States of America

07 06 05   5 4 3 2 1
First edition

This book is dedicated to all those courageous men of color from the 332nd Fighter Group who were shot down and imprisoned in the prison camps of Nazi Germany:

Name	Prison Camp	Where and When Shot Down
Lt. Edgar Bolden	Stalag Luft I	Linz, Austria
Lt. Gene Brown	Stalag Luft I	Vienna, Austria, July 18, 1944
Lt. Harold Brown	Stalag VIIA	Linz, Austria, March 4, 1944
Lt. Alfred Carroll	Stalag Luft I	Linz, Austria, July 25, 1944
Lt. Robert Daniels Jr.	Stalag Luft III and Stalag VIIA	Toulon, France, August 12, 1944
Lt. Clarence Driver	Stalag VIIA	Danube River, March 25, 1945
Lt. Thurston Gaines Jr.	Stalag VIIA	Nuremberg, Germany, April 15, 1945
Lt. Robert Gaither	Stalag VIIA	Budapest, Hungary, November 22, 1944
Lt. Newman Golden	Stalag VIIA	Linz, Austria, March 20, 1945
Lt. Alfred Gorham	Stalag VIIA	Munich, Germany, February 1945
Lt. Cornelius Gould	Stalag Luft I	Hungary, December 2, 1944
Lt. William Griffin	Stalag Luft I	Rome, Italy, January 15, 1944
Lt. Lloyd C. Hathcock	Stalag Luft III and Stalag VIIA	Rome, Italy, June 1944
Lt. Lincoln Hudson	Stalag VIIA	Tropau, Czechoslovakia, March 23, 1945
Lt. George Iles	Stalag VIIA	Munich, Germany, February 25, 1944
Lt. Alexander Jefferson	Stalag Luft III and Stalag VIIA	Toulon, France, August 12, 1944
Lt. Joe A. Lewis	Stalag Luft III and Stalag VIIA	Athens, Greece, October 6, 1944
Lt. Wilbur Long	Stalag Luft III and Stalag VIIA	Brechhammer, Poland, September 13, 1944
Lt. Richard Macon	Stalag Luft III and Stalag VIIA	Montpellier, France, August 12, 1944
Lt. Walter McCreary	Stalag Luft III and Stalag VIIA	Kaspovar, Hungary, October 22, 1944
Capt. Armour McDaniel	Stalag VIIA	Berlin, Germany, March 31, 1945
Lt. Woodrow Morgan	Stalag Luft III and Stalag VIIA	Rome, Italy, May 26, 1944
Lt. Starling Penn	Stalag Luft I	Linz, Austria, July 25, 1944
Capt. Lewis C. Smith	Stalag Luft III and Stalag VIIA	Florence, Italy, June 6, 1944
Lt. Luther Smith	Hospital and Stalag 17A	Spittal, Austria, October 13, 1944
Lt. Floyd Thompson	Stalag Luft III and Stalag VIIA	Forli, Italy, June 29, 1944

Lt. Quitman Walker		Hungary, November 22, 1944
Lt. Charles Williams	Stalag Luft III and Stalag VIIA	Yugoslavia, July 30, 1944
Lt. Kenneth Williams	Stalag Luft III and Stalag VIIA	Athens, Greece, October 4, 1944
Lt. Henry Wise	Stalag Luft I	Ploesti, Romania, August 26, 1944
Lt. Carrol S. Woods	Stalag Luft III and Stalag VIIA	Athens, Greece, October 6, 1944

Contents

Foreword

LEWIS H. CARLSON

I first met Alexander Jefferson in 1993 when I interviewed him for a book on World War II prisoners of war.[1] He was one of thirty-two Tuskegee Airmen from the 332nd Fighter Group who was shot down defending a country that still considered blacks to be second-class citizens. He, like thousands of other African Americans, including 992 Tuskegee Airmen, had fought against Hitler's racism in a military so segregated that even its blood plasma was separated by race.

I met him again several years later when he was an honored guest at the Celebrate Freedom Festival in Pigeon Forge, Tennessee. Jefferson, who had retired as a lieutenant colonel from the Air Force Reserve on July 1, 1969, happened to be the ranking officer among the several former prisoners of war being honored that day, but he was the only African American. I thought to myself, what a fascinating slice of history. Here is a man who as a young black student in Atlanta, Georgia, lived in such a racially proscribed world that he was not even allowed to walk in the city's parks. Now he is giving an inspirational address to an appreciative, overwhelmingly white audience in one of the former states of the Confederacy.

When Alexander Jefferson was commissioned a second lieutenant in the U.S. Army Air Corps in 1944, white America thought it knew its African Americans. Unfortunately, what it knew came largely from cultural stereotypes that were meant to reassure insecure whites that blacks needed to be kept firmly in their place. Black women were seen as fat, jovial Aunt Jemimas who nurtured appreciative white youngsters. Black men, on the other hand, were expected to play the "coon," afraid of their own shadow, and always clowning for the amusement of white audiences. A movie actor named Stepin Fetchit became a star in the 1930s and early 1940s playing this shuffling, lazy, chicken-stealing child-man. These same stereotypes could also be found in popular songs, novels and short stories, crude cartoons, and on weekly radio shows. In short, here was something less than a man who clearly was not ready for full citizenship, let alone capable of flying an airplane. That such images did not reflect reality mattered little to

I was treated better as a POW than I was back home.
—*Lt. Colonel Alexander Jefferson*

ix

the majority of white Americans, for whom a genuine African American, say a Tuskegee Airmen, became, in the unforgettable words of novelist Ralph Ellison, "an invisible man."

It was not only the creators of popular culture who distorted or denied the existence of millions of African Americans. Scholars and intellectuals were equally guilty. After the Civil War, white historians made it painfully clear that blacks were ill equipped to handle their newfound freedom, and, to prove their point, they portrayed the Reconstruction era as a time of misrule by carpet-baggers, scallywags, and ignorant blacks. Such an interpretation, of course, ignored the fact that many of the antebellum free blacks who returned to represent the South in state and national legislatures had been well educated, either in northern colleges or abroad, and even some of the former slaves had at least as much formal education as the old Illinois rail-splitter who became president of the United States.

Clearly, in the post–Civil War decades, it was not blacks who were unable to handle their newfound freedom, but whites, who now projected their own moral and societal shortcomings onto the object of their aversion. The result was the enforcement of a rigidly segregated society, overtly in the South, covertly in the North, that sought to control and confine the unwanted and unacceptable phenomenon of free and equal blacks.

As a further rationale for this Jim Crow America, whites also created a nostalgic view of slavery in which happy and contented blacks were clearly better off than their emancipated brethren who seemed incapable of surviving as free Americans. Joel Chandler Harris's invention of the wise and kindly Uncle Remus was typical, as were the many maudlin songs of Stephen Foster and, several decades later, the unforgettable plantation images of Margaret Mitchell's *Gone with the Wind* and its many imitators. This 3-M interpretation of slavery, with all its moonlight, magnolia blossoms, and sticky molasses, also found acceptance among many white historians, and not all of them Southerners. Slavery, concluded U. B. Phillips, a prominent Georgia-born white historian who taught at the Universities of Michigan, Wisconsin, and Yale in the early twentieth century, although not necessarily an admirable institution, was nevertheless the "best school" for developing "a fairly efficient body of laborers out of a horde of savages." As late as the 1950 edition of their textbook *The Growth of the American Republic*, Henry Steele Commager and Samuel Eliot Morison, two of America's most distinguished and widely read liberal, Northern historians, wrote, "As for Sambo, whose wrongs moved the abolitionists to wrath and tears, there is some reason to believe that he suffered less than any other class in the South from its 'peculiar institution.'"[2]

Similarly, prominent scientists in the early twentieth century were equally convinced that blacks were permanently trapped on the lower rungs of the evolutionary ladder. To prove the point, in 1906 the New York Zoological Society placed an African pigmy by the name of Ota Benga and an orangutan together in a cage. In 1927, Yale geographer Ellsworth Huntington wrote, "[Negroes] and their slavery have been enemies to the children of the Builders," while in the same year Harvard geneticist Edward East concluded, "Mentally the African negro [sic] is childlike, normally affable and cheerful, but subject to fits of fierce passion. . . . We can find no probability that the negro will contribute hereditary factors of value to the white race." And for the University of Virginia's Robert Bennett Bean, writing in 1935, "The size of the brain in the Black Race is below the medium both of the Whites and of the Yellow-Browns."[3]

That such pseudoscience and deformed history reflected preconceived notions of racial superiority rather than scholarly research or empirical evidence seems obvious today, but often overlooked is how such distorted thinking adversely affected African Americans' historic struggle for civil rights and professional opportunities, regardless of their individual and collective accomplishments. The history of African American participation in military service is a case in point.

In spite of the resistance of military and political leaders, African Americans have willingly, and often heroically, fought and died in every American military conflict, going as far back as the eighteenth-century skirmishes and wars against the Indians, French, and, of course, the British. Unfortunately, 250 years of military duty and sacrifice have all too often been ignored, or else trivialized by allowing a heroic name or two to creep into the record. Crispus Attucks, who died in the 1770 Boston Massacre, comes immediately to mind, but playing a much greater role in the colonial struggle for independence were the five thousand free and enslaved blacks who fought in the Continental Army, various state militias, and the budding American navy. To be sure, fighting for a fledgling government that sanctioned slavery was a difficult decision, and there were those African Americans who joined the British loyalists in return for the promise of freedom. Indeed, it was such promises by the British that forced George Washington and his generals to reverse their earlier policy of opposing the enlistment of blacks.

The contributions of African American soldiers and sailors in the Revolutionary War helped fuel the abolitionist movement in the North, leading to the end of slavery in several northern states, but they did not result in equal opportunities in the military. After the war the army restricted itself to a small number of black scouts and guides, and in 1798 the newly formed U.S. Marine Corps totally excluded "Negroes, mulattos, and Indians."

Initially, the navy afforded African Americans more and better opportunities than did the army, largely because of a shortage of willing white recruits and because many white sailors, appalled by the living conditions aboard the ships, deserted. Blacks fought in the Barbary Wars of 1801–1805 and in the War of 1812, where approximately 10 percent of the sailors were black. Of the fifty black seamen who fought with him at the Battle of Lake Erie, Captain Oliver H. Perry said, "They seemed absolutely insensible to danger."[4] In the Civil War, one in every four of the 118,000 Union sailors was black, and at least four were awarded the Medal of Honor.[5] In spite of such promising beginnings, the subsequent status of African Americans in the U.S. Navy steadily declined until by World Wars I and II they were allowed to serve only as stewards or messmen. The navy's top brass explained this decision by insisting that blacks lacked the mental and technical abilities to master the technology of the modern navy.

Relatively few black soldiers participated in the land battles of the War of 1812, but General Andrew Jackson promised those who fought with him in the Battle of New Orleans that "the American nation shall applaud your valor, as your general now praises your ardor."[6] Unfortunately, such was not the case, and an 1820 U.S. Army order prohibited any further recruitment of blacks.

The Civil War provided an enormous opportunity for African American soldiers again to prove their mettle. Inspired by Frederick Douglass, who promised that "slaves and free colored people [would form] a liberating army, to march into the South and raise the banner of emancipation among the slaves,"[7] thousands of African Americans eagerly sought to enlist. Initially, Lincoln refused to use black troops, fearing they would prove inadequate and that "half the Army would lay down their arms and three other states would join the rebellion."[8] Despite Lincoln's reticence, many slaves abruptly fled their masters and joined the invading Northern forces, usually serving in support roles or as sentries. Finally, after flagging enlistments, mounting casualties, and increasing pressure from abolitionists forced the president's hand, Lincoln agreed in 1862 to the enlistment of African Americans.

More than 183,000 African Americans served in the Union army. Called the United States Colored Troops (USCT), 93,000 of them came from the slave states, thereby contradicting those white Southerners who insisted their slaves were content with the "Peculiar Institution." Another 40,000 came from the border states, and the remaining 53,000 from the free states. After 1862, blacks fought in every major campaign, serving in the infantry, cavalry, and artillery and as engineers and scouts. More than 38,000 lost their lives, a mortality rate nearly 40 percent higher than that suffered by their white counterparts.

Most celebrated was the 54th Massachusetts Volunteers, whose march into Charleston, South Carolina, was immortalized 124 years later, not in traditional history books but in Edward Zwick's 1989 movie *Glory*. Other black units also made significant contributions to the Union cause, but such wartime heroics did not translate into peacetime opportunities, and the only black units to remain on active duty after the cessation of hostilities were the 24th and 25th Infantry and the 9th and 10th Cavalry Regiments, later known as the Buffalo Soldiers for their exploits on the frontier fighting Indians.

The Buffalo Soldiers also played a prominent role in the Spanish American War; in fact, the 10th Cavalry, under Captain John J. Pershing, known as "Black Jack" for his leadership of African American troops, may well have reached the top of San Juan Hill before Col. Theodore Roosevelt's renowned Rough Riders. Indeed, they fought so well that one Southern-born white officer later admitted, "If it had not been for the Negro cavalry the Rough Riders would have been exterminated."[9]

Black soldiers also fought against the Philippine insurgents between 1899 and 1902, but in spite of their recurring military accomplishments, their treatment had not noticeably improved by 1917, when the United States entered World War I to make the world safe for democracy.

Although still barred from the Marines and not allowed in the Army's Aviation Corps, more than 367,000 African Americans served in World War I. All served in segregated units, except for those fortunate enough to fight with the French.

The first black soldiers to land in Europe worked primarily as laborers and stevedores. The first combat unit was the 369th Infantry, assigned to the French, who welcomed them as fellow soldiers rather than as porters needed to carry or clean equipment. From April 1918 until the end of the war—191 straight days on the front lines—the 369th conducted itself as admirably as any American unit in Europe. They were the first Allied troops to reach the Rhine, and they never lost a man to capture or ever retreated in the face of German attacks. The Germans called them "Hell Fighters," and the French awarded the entire regiment the Croix de Guerre and honored 171 of its individual soldiers with either the Croix de Guerre or the Legion of Honor.

The 370th, 371st, and 372nd Infantry Regiments were also assigned to the French "Red Hand" Division. Along with the 369th, their accomplishments were such that French General Goybet proudly proclaimed, "These crack regiments overcame every obstacle with a most complete contempt for danger. . . . Through their steady devotion, the "Red Hand Division" . . . was constantly leading the way for the victorious advance of the Fourth Army."[10]

Unfortunately, once again wartime achievements did not result in improved conditions for blacks, either in the military or on the home front. In August 1918, a document titled *Secret Information Concerning Black Troops* warned the French that intermingling with black troops would lead to the assault and rape of white women. That the French ignored such advice simply made white Americans more determined than ever to reassert their control over the lives and destinies of African Americans once the country returned to normalcy.

The returning Expeditionary troops were enthusiastically welcomed by huge parades in many northern cities, and scattered among them were several black units, but their moment of glory was short-lived. Triggered by the Red Scare, a resurgent nativism, a revitalized Ku Klux Klan, and a lack of leadership in Washington, these postwar years were among the most racially violent in American history. President Woodrow Wilson, who even before the war had issued an executive order segregating all government offices, restaurants, and restrooms, as well as effectively eliminating blacks from the civil service, was certainly not going to encourage domestic civil and economic rights after the armistice. More than a hundred blacks were lynched in 1919 and 1920, including many former soldiers, some of whom were still proudly wearing their uniforms. Over the next few years deadly race riots broke out in both northern and southern cities, the worst of which occurred in Chicago in July 1919, when fifteen whites and twenty-three blacks lost their lives, and two years later in Tulsa, when twenty-one blacks and nine whites were killed. The racial climate had scarcely improved, when, on October 30, 1925, the War Department distributed a memo titled *The Use of Negro Man Power in War*. Totally ignoring African Americans long and often illustrious record in combat, the War Department argued that the black soldier be restricted to maintenance units because he "was physically unqualified for combat duty [and was] by nature subservient, mentally inferior, and believed himself to be inferior to the white man." In addition, he was "susceptible to the influence of crowd psychology, could not control himself in the face of danger, and did not have the initiative and resourcefulness of the white man."[11]

In September 1940, in preparation for an even more deadly and destructive world war, Congress enacted the Selective Training and Service Act. Reacting to increasing African American demands for a more equitable role in the military, this first peacetime draft called for blacks to be trained for combat, but only in segregated units. The U.S. Army Air Corps, which in World War I had rejected all African American applicants because "it was impossible to mix blacks with whites,"[12] now grudgingly admitted blacks, although also only in segregated units. A War Department memo sent to President Roosevelt on October 8, 1940, rationalized this decision, arguing that experimenting with integrated units "would produce situations destructive to morale and detrimental to the preparations for national defense."[13] From these contrary but fateful decisions emerged the Tuskegee experiment to train black pilots.

More than three million African Americans registered for the draft and approximately one million served on active duty, but the question persisted: Would their fighting abilities be fully utilized and would their military achievements translate into a more open society for all blacks in postwar America? Looking back after the passage of more than a half century, one has to conclude that the government's response was more positive and proactive than it ever had been in the past.

President Truman took the first steps. The 1947 report of his Civil Rights Commission, *To Secure These Rights*, concluded, "The war experiences brought to our attention a laboratory in which we may prove that the majority and minorities of our population can train and work and fight side by side in cooperation and harmony."[14] The next year Truman issued Executive Order 9981, mandating the integration of the armed forces. Clearly, the achievements of the Tuskegee Airmen and other black combatants played a pivotal role in the president's decision, as they did in advancing the civil rights movement of the 1950s, but the struggle was never smooth or easy. The U.S. Army and the Marines still went into battle in the Korean War in segregated units, although battlefield necessities often forced the intermixing of white and black troops. Not until September 1954 was the secretary of defense able to announce that the last all-black unit had been abolished. Another important step was taken in July 1963 when Secretary of Defense Robert McNamara ordered the elimination of off-base discrimination. Thereafter, the armed services' record in affording African Americans fair and equal career opportunities has matched or exceeded anything found in the civilian sector.

For years after the end of World War II, the majority of Americans, including many African Americans, had no idea that black fighter pilots fought in World War II, let alone that they had such a sterling record of achievement. And even after learning of the heroic exploits of the Tuskegee Airmen, it was difficult for most white Americans to put aside the pervasive stereotypes that had clouded their judgment. Where, they wondered, had the Air Corps found men of this caliber? Surely not from among all those eye-rolling, shuffling Amos-and-Andy characters with which they were so familiar. Simply put, most white Americans had never seen, let alone met, a black physician, educator, lawyer, or pilot.

There were, of course, as Alexander Jefferson's story makes clear, thousands of African American families with academic and professional pedigrees just as impressive as those found in the white community. In fact, the average Tuskegee Airman had better academic credentials than his white counterpart. Jefferson, who came from a long line of prominent clergymen and educators, was typical. He had completed undergraduate majors in biology and chemistry and had taken graduate courses in chemistry. In addition, he had worked as a chemist before joining the Tuskegee program and also exhibited considerable artistic talents.

As exceptional as many of the African American pilots were, their struggle for acceptance was never easy. West Point graduate Benjamin O. Davis Jr., who was in the first graduating class of Tuskegee Airmen in 1942, well understood the challenges of surviving and overcoming the racist individuals and institutions that wanted him to fail. As had been the case with earlier blacks who had attended the U.S. Military Academy, his fellow cadets not only refused to room with him but also gave him the "silent treatment," never speaking to him during his four years of study. However, such affronts only made this future lieutenant general more determined. He wrote, "All the blacks in the segregated forces operated like they had to prove they could fly an airplane when everyone believed they were too stupid. [But] we would go through any ordeal that came our way, be it in garrison existence or combat, to prove our worth."[15]

Archie Williams was one of the few black instructors at the Tuskegee Army Air Field. He possessed three university degrees, including one in engineering from the University of California, Berkeley, and an Olympic gold medal, won in the 400-meter dash at the 1936 Berlin Olympics. Williams knew white America expected his students to fail, but he also knew that this would not be the case. With tongue-in-cheek drollery, he noted, "After all, we were the cream of the crop."

> We knew the whites in charge figured, "We'll get these niggers in a bunch of airplanes and let them kill themselves, and that will be that." But the funny part of it was that they skimmed the cream of the crop out of the colleges. We had guys with PhDs, physicians, engineers–two of them even became four-star generals. These guys were hand-picked, so there was no way we were going to flop.[16]

Archie Williams was right. The 450 Tuskegee-trained fighter pilots of the 99th Fighter Squadron and the 332nd Fighter Group flew more than 15,000 sorties and 1,500 missions over North Africa and Europe. During their more than two hundred missions, which involved escorting bombers to and from their targets, the Red-Tail Angels, as the custom-painted P-51 Mustangs of the 332nd were affectionately called by the bomber crews they were protecting, never lost a single bomber to enemy aircraft. They were also credited with damaging or destroying 409 German aircraft and even one destroyer. Sixty-six of these brave men were killed in combat, and another thirty-two, including Alexander Jefferson, were shot down and became prisoners of war.

Even after proving themselves in combat against the Luftwaffe, Jefferson and his fellow Tuskegee Airmen returned to a country that continued to treat them as second-class citizens. Consider the humiliation, as Jefferson describes it, of coming down the gangplank in the shadow of the Statue of Liberty and being ordered by a young, white private, "Whites to the right, niggers to the left."

Of course, American society would eventually change, and the armed forces have certainly been in the vanguard in offering increasingly attractive career opportunities for African Americans. Much slower has been the civilian sector, but here too social and economic possibilities gradually improved, at least for the black middle class and the former Tuskegee Airmen.

In retrospect, the Tuskegee Airmen were indeed heroic warriors—the Germans called them *Schwarze Vogelmenschen*, or Black Birdmen, but their achievements were not limited to the battlefields of World War II. After returning home, some became very successful in the civilian sector. Others stayed in the military and played important roles in integrating the armed forces, including two who became four-star generals and one who earned three stars. Without exception, all continued their struggle for civil rights, and not just for African Americans, as Alexander Jefferson once explained, "but for all humankind in the United States."

NOTES

1. Lewis H. Carlson, *We Were Each Other's Prisoners: An Oral History of World War II American and German Prisoners of War* (New York: Basic Books, 1997).

2. Lewis H. Carlson and George A. Colburn, *In Their Place: White America Defines Her Minorities, 1850–1950* (New York: John Wiley & Sons, 1972), 107–8.

3. Ibid., 99–106.

4. John Hope Franklin, *From Slavery to Freedom: A History of Negro Americans* (New York: Knopf, 1947, 1997), 124.

5. Lerone Bennett Jr., *Before the Mayflower: A History of Black America, 1619–1962*, 4th ed. (Chicago: Johnson, 1969), 394.

6. Ibid., 125.

7. David Herbert Donald, *Lincoln* (New York: Simon & Schuster, 1995), 367.

8. Ibid.

9. Franklin, *From Slavery to Freedom*, 310.

10. Ibid., 345.

11. "The Use of Negro Man Power in War," 30 October 1925, Albert F. Simpson Historical Research Center, MAFB; quoted in Alan Osur, *Blacks in the Army Air Forces During*

World War II: The Problem of Race Relations (Washington, DC: U.S. Government Printing Office, 1977), 2.

12. William Alexander Percy, "Jim Crow and Uncle Sam: The Tuskegee Flying Units and the U.S. Army Air Forces in Europe During World War II," *The Journal of Military History* 67 (July 2003), 775.

13. Ibid., 776.

14. Ibid., 810.

15. Quoted in General Benjamin O. Davis's obituary, *New York Times*, July 7, 2002.

16. Personal interview. See also Lewis H. Carlson and John J. Fogarty, *Tales of Gold: An Oral History of the Summer Olympic Games Told by America's Gold Medal Winners* (Chicago: Contemporary Books, 1987), 144–58.

Alexander Jefferson Timeline

November 15, 1921	Alexander Jefferson is born in Detroit, Michigan
June 1938	Graduates from Detroit's Chadsey High School
September 1938	Begins Clark College in Atlanta, Georgia
June 1942	Graduates from Clark College with majors in chemistry and biology and minors in mathematics and physics, and returns to Detroit
September 23, 1942	Sworn into the U.S. Army Reserves
September 1942	Begins graduate school at Howard University in Washington, D.C.
April 13, 1943	Called to active duty to begin flight training
May 2–July 1, 1943	Preflight training at Tuskegee Army Air Field
July 2–September 1, 1943	Primary flight training at Tuskegee Institute
September 2–November 1, 1943	Basic Flight Training at Tuskegee Army Air Field
Nov. 2, 1943–Jan. 6, 1944	Advanced flight training at Tuskegee Army Air Field
January 7, 1944	Graduation. Receives his wings as a second lieutenant in the U.S. Army Air Corps
January 7–February 5, 1944	P-40 training at Tuskegee Army Air Field
February 5–May 10, 1944	Training in P-39s at Selfridge Army Air Base, Detroit
May 12–May 26, 1944	Training in P-39s at Walterboro Army Air Field, South Carolina
May 27–June 8, 1944	En route to overseas assignment
June 8–13, 1944	Oran, Algeria
June 15–June 19, 1944	Naples, Italy
June 20–August 12, 1944	Ramitelli Air Base in southern Italy, combat replacement pilot in the all-black 332nd Fighter Group
August 12, 1944	Shot down over southern France; becomes a POW
August 18–20, 1944	Oberursel, Germany, near Frankfurt
August 20–23, 1944	Dulag Luft, Wetzler, Germany, for interrogation
August 26, 1944	Arrives in Stalag Luft III at Sagan, Germany
January 27, 1945	Evacuates Stalag Luft III
February 3, 1945	Arrives in Stalag VIIA at Moosburg, Germany
April 29, 1945	Liberation

June 7, 1945	Arrives in New York
June 7–August 18, 1945	Leave, processing, and reassignment, Atlantic City, New Jersey
August 15–January 1, 1946	Instrument and flying instructor, Tuskegee Army Air Field
October 16, 1946	Marries Adella McDonald-Tucker
January 16, 1947	Discharged from active duty; joins the Air Force Reserve
September 1947–June 1948	Takes science education classes and earns a teaching certificate at Detroit's Wayne State University
September 1948	Begins teaching science at Duffield Elementary School in Detroit
June 1953	Receives M.A. in education from Wayne State University
September 1954	Moves to Pattengill Elementary School in Detroit
June 1, 1960	Completes thirty hours of graduate work in education beyond his M.A.
September 9, 1969	Becomes assistant principal of Detroit's Halley Elementary School
July 1, 1969	Retires from the Air Force Reserve with a rank of Lt. Colonel
September 1970	Becomes assistant principal at Detroit's Ferry Elementary School
July 12, 1972	One of the organizers of the Detroit Chapter of the Tuskegee Airmen, the first such chapter in the United States
July 1974–July 1996	Serves as president of the Detroit chapter of the Tuskegee Airmen
1978–present	Serves as a voluntary admissions counselor for the U.S. Air Force Academy and the U.S. Air Force Reserve Officer Training Corps
June 1979	Retires from the Detroit Public Schools
October 14, 1995	Enshrined in the Michigan Aviation Hall of Fame at the Kalamazoo Air Museum in Kalamazoo, Michigan

Red Tail Captured, Red Tail Free

A model P-51 Mustang Red Tail, constructed by Alexander Jefferson.

Introduction

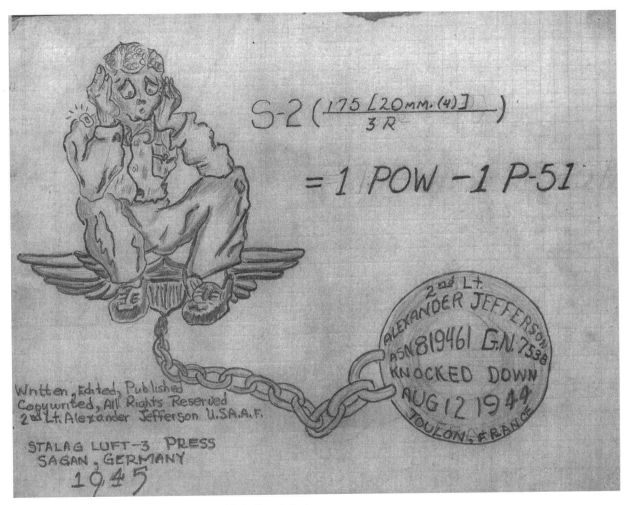

Alexander Jefferson sitting on his wings with ball and chain.

Two World War II dates live in infamy for me. The first, December 7, 1941, I share with all my fellow citizens. The second is much more personal. On August 12, 1944, I was a proud member of the 332nd Fighter Group, later known as the Tuskegee Airmen. I was flying my P-51 on a strafing run over southern France. It was my nineteenth and final mission.

For the next nine months I was a guest of the Third Reich. Actually, I was a *Kriegie*, which stands for *Kriegsgefangene*, meaning prisoner of war. I was not held prisoner as long as many others were, but conditions were sufficiently challenging that I needed a diversion to keep my mind occupied. I started drawing the sketches that appear throughout this book after my arrival in Stalag Luft III on August 20, 1944, and I continued drawing them until we were liberated from Stalag VIIA on April 29, 1945. Because no cameras were available, I hoped that my drawings, which I drew on pale, yellow paper supplied by the International Red Cross, would document both my combat experiences as a fighter pilot and the frustrations I endured as a prisoner of war.

My love of drawing and flying went back to my earliest years. In fact, I cannot remember a time when I was not drawing or making model airplanes. The smell of model plane glue still permeates my senses. I put together every known model imaginable. My masterpiece was a super Marine Spitfire with twin two-foot floats and a three-foot wingspan. I drew the plans from newspaper photos. One of my most disheartening moments came in 1945. I had just arrived home from overseas, only to discover that my parents had thrown away my Marine Spitfire and all my modeling tools.

As a boy, I was also fascinated by a buck-toothed, rule breaking, daredevil World War I pilot named Phineus Pinkham, who was always in some kind of trouble when he wasn't shooting down German planes. I read about his breath-taking exploits and those of other fighter pilots in a magazine called *Flying Aces*, and I dreamed of the day I would be performing my own heroic deeds.

By the time I arrived at Stalag Luft III, it had become a camp primarily for captured British and American Air Force officers. It was located just south of Sagan, approximately ninety miles southeast of Berlin in what is now southwestern Poland. The Luftwaffe administered the camp, and we were not overtly mistreated. As a result, many of my sketches appear lighthearted, even whimsical, but life for a prisoner was never that easy. It was simply too dangerous for me to draw a German sentry taking a shot at a POW reaching for a ball that had rolled under the warning wire or a guard shooting and killing a prisoner who was standing in the doorway of his barracks. It was equally difficult, if not impossible, to sketch what it meant to stand for hours in subzero weather while the guards searched our barracks for *Kriegie* contraband or the endless hours of unmitigated hunger and boredom and those interminable nights spent longing for loved ones we were never quite sure we would see again.

While I was a prisoner, I also wrote down observations in a small notebook that, toward the end of my incarceration, became a running log on what was happening to us, especially after we were forced to evacuate Stalag Luft III and make the long trek to Stalag VIIA in Moosburg, Germany. Without these notations, there is no way I could have recalled the many details of that bitterly cold march and our final days before liberation.

I began writing this memoir in 1948 when I became an elementary school science teacher in Detroit. Aviation was the general theme of my classroom, and I had several model planes hanging from the ceiling. When these ten- and eleven-year-old black kids asked me, "Mr. Jefferson, what did you do during the war?" I would tell them, "I was there." Then I would describe how I felt living the life of a raunchy, daredevil fighter pilot and what it was like to be a "Negro" U.S. Army Air Corps pilot in these United States between 1943 and 1946. Over the ensuing decades, I continued to write down my recollections. Now I am eighty-three years old, and it is time to finish the job.

Tuskegee Airman Buy War Bonds poster.

1 Detroit The Formative Years

I was born in Detroit, Michigan, on November 15, 1921, the first child of Alexander Jefferson and Jane White Jefferson. My parents had only recently moved to Detroit from Atlanta, Georgia, because there were factory jobs to be had in the Motor City. They would have two more children, my sister Emma, who was born on March 25, 1925, and my brother Clarence, born on November 7, 1930.

My mother was born in 1891 in Newnan, Georgia, just southwest of Atlanta, into a prominent family that had long made its mark in religious and educational circles. Her paternal grandfather, William Jefferson White, was born in the 1830s to a slave woman and a white man, but he was never a slave. He became a minister of the Springfield Baptist Church in Augusta, Georgia, where, in 1867, he opened a school in the church basement that he called Augusta Institute. This small, black, all-male school, which initially trained its students exclusively for the ministry and pedagogy, later moved to Atlanta. Over the years, it changed its name to Atlanta Baptist Seminary, Atlanta Baptist College, and finally, early in the twentieth century, Morehouse College. Today, Morehouse is a nationally and internationally respected liberal arts and medical school that offers a wide variety of majors to students from more than forty states and eighteen foreign countries. Dr. Martin Luther King Jr. is one of Morehouse's most famous graduates.

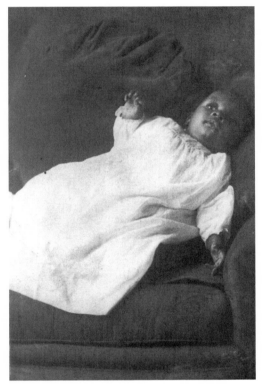

Alexander Jefferson, age six months.

William Jefferson White had two families. One was legitimate, while the other, shall we say, existed in a backroom. I don't know much about the background of this second family, except the woman in the backroom, who was a slave and seamstress in the master's house, gave birth to my grandfather, Henry Montgomery White, who became a very prominent Atlanta clergyman, and with whom I lived during my undergraduate college days. After Henry graduated in

Alexander Jefferson,
age two years.

1880 from Clark University, and later completed his studies at Gammon Theological Seminary, he became pastor of the South Atlanta Methodist Church, which is now known as the Henry Montgomery White United Methodist Church. His wife, Emma Nelson White, graduated from Atlanta University in 1885, and their daughter, Jane, became my mother.

Of course, we have no birth certificate, but we know that when my Grandfather White died in 1954 he was more than a hundred years old. When he lay on his deathbed, my mother remembers him ranting deliriously, reliving the horror of seeing his mother beaten by the master because she was somehow to blame when he and the master's son got into some type of trouble. At the time, the two boys were only twelve or thirteen. The master had evidently become so angry that he tied her hands, suspended her from a rafter in the barn, and whipped her.

My mother graduated from Clark in 1910 with a degree in pedagogy, which consisted of the art, methods, and principles of the teaching profession. She then taught school in Newnan until she married my father in 1920. Her two sisters, Lydia and Dorothy, were also graduates of Clark. Their parents stressed the importance of education, which would enable them to escape domestic service in a white man's household where they would be subject to mental and physical abuse.

Although Grandfather White had his college and seminary degrees and Grandmother Emma White was also a college graduate, they did not encourage any of their four sons, Henry Jr., Maceo, Charles, and Walter, to pursue higher education. Instead, they were encouraged to pursue manual trades as carpenters, mechanics, and handymen.

My father was born on March 25, 1880, near Lynchburg, in central South Carolina. His father, Fortune Jefferson, had been born a slave in 1832, which means I am only two generations removed from slavery on both sides of my family. Fortune Jefferson was a very prolific man. My father was the tenth of eleven children. His mother, Susan Boone Jefferson, died giving birth to her twelfth child in 1890. Fortune then married seventeen-year-old Rosa Lee Thomas and proceeded to have seven more children. He ran a blacksmith shop in Lynch-burg until he died in 1911.

There was nothing for a young black man to do around Lynchburg, except sharecropping, so in 1916 my father left to seek employment in Atlanta where he met my mother. Two years later, he went to Detroit and secured a job as a laborer at the Detroit Lubricator Company, which was owned by a black man named Eliza McCoy. My father worked for Detroit Lubricator the rest of his life, and although he joined the union, he remained a staunch Republican, simply because, he said, "They freed the slaves."

My father returned to Atlanta in 1920 to marry my mother, after which they immediately returned to Detroit. My father only finished the eighth grade, but he was a whiz with mathematical figures. I remember him sitting in his wooden rocker behind our isinglass stove and the orange peel aroma of Prince Albert tobacco rising from his pipe and filling the entire house. He would sit for hours, his lap filled with papers, systematically rotating, adding, subtracting, and ma-nipulating numbers until finally he produced what he considered "the number" for the day, which he often hit.

Mother was a rigid moralist. As the product of a Methodist minister father and a university-educated mother, she was a real "MK" (minister's kid) and al-ways very proper. She did not dance, and she drank nothing stronger than lem-onade. But she was also an intellectual who had been greatly influenced by the professors at Clark University, where, among other things, she had studied Greek and Latin.

Dad, on the other hand, was very, very different. At least before they married, he loved to dance and have a good time. He was also a sharp dresser and enjoyed an occasional drink, although he had to keep his bottle of gin out in the barn. I discovered this only after I returned from the service, and he took me out back and offered me a drink to welcome me home!

My mother did not know he played the numbers. A couple of times a week he would secretly risk a few pennies with Keyser, the numbers man, a young Polish guy who lived right behind us. I'm not sure, but I think the payoff was five hundred to one, which meant for every penny bet, one might win five dollars.

My father was extremely hard working. During the long years of the Depres-sion, he was fortunate to be the only man on our entire block who had a job. I can still see him walking home from the Buchanan Street trolley, swinging his

[left]
Jane White Jefferson,
mother.
[right]
Alexander Jefferson,
father.

lunch pail and greeting all the neighbor men on their front steps and them responding, "Hi, Mr. Jefferson."

My father was also an unofficial "railroad conductor" for many of our relatives in the twenties and thirties who came north from Lynchburg, South Carolina, and Atlanta, Georgia, looking for better lives. I can remember a steady stream of aunts and uncles moving me out of my bed and onto a cot or a wood pallet on the floor and having to run down to the corner store to get more groceries. My father was their financial support until they could find work and secure their own place to rent.

Our address in Detroit was 4014 28th Street, and initially the house consisted of two, side-by-side "shotgun" units. We lived in the north side unit of four rooms. The front room was the parlor, which featured our piano. The next room was Mom and Dad's bedroom. One step down was my bedroom, and another step down was the kitchen, with a corner blocked off for the toilet. The sink was on the other side of the toilet, facing the stove. In back was our barn, one side of which had room for a car and the other side contained bins for coal and coke.

Aunt Mame and Uncle Gee lived in the four-room unit on the other side of us. When they moved out in 1926, Dad cut two doors through the wall, so we then had an eight-room house. Our old kitchen became the bathroom, our parlor became Mom and Dad's bedroom, their bedroom became my sister Emma's bedroom, the room opposite my bedroom became the dining room, and in the room opposite Emma's bedroom there was a large isinglass baseburner stove that heated the front six rooms.

One of my earliest memories of that house is the smell of boiling coffee at 4:00 a.m. Then I'd hear my father slam the door, and I'd go back to sleep. A couple of hours later I faced the stark reality of getting up, washing my face in cold water, and eating shredded wheat with cold milk, even on the coldest winter days. But we never went hungry, and we never ate plain hamburger. Mr. Parsons, who was the owner and butcher at the corner store, would cut off strips of tenderloin and grind it for us. I thought that T-bone steak was part of a regular meal. There was sawdust on the store floor, and on the counter were huge jars of pickles and open spice containers that gave off a rich aroma. I remember Mr. Parson scooping peanut butter out of a large tub into a paper container. The oil would leak through, and in a few days the peanut butter would be as hard as a brick.

Then there was the C. F. Smith Bakery, where I would go to buy bread. It was about ten blocks away on West Grand Boulevard, just south of Michigan Avenue, under the railroad viaduct. I could smell the heavenly aroma of the ovens the entire ten blocks. Bread was then five cents a loaf, uncut and fresh out of the oven. I'd sometimes buy an extra loaf, scoop out the inside, and just eat the crust! Fantastically delicious! No one today would dream of allowing a seven- or eight-year-old to walk up Jackson Street to the Boulevard, go under the railroad tracks, then onto Michigan Avenue.

One of our summer rituals was to fill several open-mouthed gallon jugs with peaches and then cover them with sugar. We would put the jugs next to the chimney, where the heat would proceed to do its duty. We were always told that the "juice" was a home remedy for medicinal purposes, such as winter coughs and colds. I do know it sure tasted good!

When the weather turned really cold, we heated bricks next to the baseburner and put them under the blankets of our beds. The blankets were heavy, wool army blankets or comforters made by my mother from odd pieces of old clothing. The kitchen stove was a combination coal and wood stove, with a warmer on top. Food must have been different back then because sweet potatoes stayed in the warmer day and night and never spoiled. The wood and coal stove kept the kitchen and dining room warm. There was also a gas heater, with a door that you had to open and ignite the gas with a match. I recall forgetting to turn off the gas one day and the tank overheated and almost burst.

Coal was then $4.00 a ton and was delivered directly through the alley to the coal bins in the barn. I was often responsible for directing the deliveryman to put the coal into the correct bin. Coke went into one bin, used at night to bank the fire, and hard coal went into the other bin. If they got mixed, I caught hell. It was also my responsibility to carry the coal into the house in a scuttle and to take out the ashes in the morning and evening. I dumped the ashes in the back-yard. In the spring we turned the ashes into the soil and raised the biggest and best collards you have ever seen.

Dish Night was a big event in our neighborhood. To get your free dish, you went to the Buchanan Theater on Friday night and on Saturday to the Crystal Theater on Michigan Avenue. The price of admission was a nickel, and for this you received a piece of pottery or cutlery. Of course, we would also catch up on the newsreels and the latest Mickey Mouse cartoons. Sometimes the Crystal would offer two dishes for the price of one admission. Much of our everyday dinnerware came from these two theaters.

My parents never owned an automobile or learned to drive. We traveled by bus or streetcar. I didn't own a store-bought shirt until I got in the army. My mother made my shirts, as well as my sister's clothes. I ironed my own clothes. I also helped with the canning of fruits and vegetables and with the baking and quilt making.

The Detroit of my youth was very conservative and very safe. Doors were left unlocked, but we kids never had free reign in the neighborhood. If I did some-thing wrong, the neighbors were not above punishing me. Of course, news of what I had done got back home faster than I did, so when I got back home, I could expect even more trouble because whatever I had done was an insult to my family's reputation.

We lived in a Polish neighborhood, except for the occasional Jewish family. The majority of these Poles were from the old country, and one of my fondest memories is the delicious potato pancakes they used to make. Our next-door neighbor to the south was the Wonokowskis, and to the north lived the Jankowskis. The Jankowskis had a boy my age named Jiggs and an older brother, Phil, who always kept his right hand in his pocket because he had injured it working at Kelsey Hayes. They also had two girls: Eleanor was a tomboy, who played baseball in the alley better than any boy, and Cecelia, whom we knew as "See Law."

The Polish youngsters attended St. Hedwich, which was the local Polish Catholic church. I'm not sure what we thought of the Catholic religion. I do know that I never attended church with them or they with me. I also sensed that their parents did not completely approve of my sister and me. After years of living side by side, Mrs. Jankowski revealed, somewhat apologetically in her broken English, that her priest had instructed her never to have anything to do with "colored" people. The Jankowskis were very, very poor. I was astonished when the children came out of the house with a piece of bread, smeared with lard, and sprinkled with sugar. They considered this a once-a-week treat. An orange, they told me, was something you looked forward to only at Christmas.

The Poles referred to a Jewish man who lived two blocks away on Jackson Street, between Lovett and Scotten, as "The Sheenie Man." He rode a horse-drawn wagon through the alleys, picking up and buying junk. I saw the hatred and resentment the Poles felt for him, but this "Sheenie Man" educated both sons to become doctors.

When I was thirteen or fourteen, I worked for the "Sheenie Man" for about a year. He had a Model T truck, and I got the job of driving it up and down the alleys. We scavenged or bought copper wire, aluminum pots and pans, paper, iron, and steel. Burning the insulation off the copper wire was my job, and the smell of that acrid smoke still comes to my nostrils whenever I think of him.

A very fair "colored" woman named Mrs. Clark lived across the street from us. Her equally light-skinned husband walked every morning to the streetcar line dressed in coat, shirt, and tie, and carrying a small satchel. He was said to have a job as a barber in a downtown hotel. We never considered them to be

Negroes, because they lived apart from us until their grandson came to visit. His name was Martin Jenkins, and years later he helped me get into graduate school at Howard University.

My mother had an extensive library. I recall sitting on the floor completely engrossed in the wooden engraved illustrations I found in *Les Misérables*. I also remember reading to myself at a very young age. Daily newspapers were a very important part of the daily routine in our house, and my sister and I always fought over the funnies, until my dad insisted that we read the headlines to him. I thought that was kind of lazy of him, but it became a fascinating game. He would wait until I had read several headlines, and then ask me, "What was the second headline. . . . Don't look!"

School was always easy for me, and never much of a challenge. I was double promoted twice in elementary school. I went to kindergarten at the old Newberry Elementary School a block away, in a structure that was built about 1895. Then, while the new Newberry School was being constructed, I walked to the first grade at Craft Elementary on Vinewood and Michigan Avenues, approximately two miles from our house.

My third-grade teacher, Mrs. Laidlaw, gave me hell. To avoid her wrath, I always finished my lessons before anyone else, so she didn't know what to do with me. My sixth-grade teacher, Mrs. Simpson, was an austere, unsmiling disciplinarian. Try as I might, I could never outmaneuver her. She was always one step ahead of me, and I learned to appreciate and respect her. I know she was responsible for greatly improving my English.

As the oldest child in the family and being male, I was aware at a very early age that I was a Negro. I remember going downtown to Hudson's Department Store with my mother when I was five or six and noticing that the only blacks working there were very fair-skinned women. They held the auspicious position of elevator operators and wore black uniforms with lacy white aprons. I also knew there were restaurants in Detroit that did not serve blacks. My mother introduced me to this fact by saying, "We can't stop here," and I somehow understood that the reason was our color.

I also had to walk home from school through "foreign" territory, which meant Polish or Jewish. There were often racial slurs and indignities, and one thing would lead to another. This meant I had to run or pick up a two-by-four or a rock or use my fists and fight my way home. Nevertheless, until I was in my teens I was accepted by the Polish boys in my immediate neighborhood. They would even fight to protect me when we ventured out of the neighborhood.

We were the 28th Street Gang, and I was the only black member. I still remember some of their names: "Frenchie" was my age; "Keyser," who lived behind us on Jackson Street, was several years older and ran the numbers; "Bed Bug" lived up the block from us; "Jiggs" lived next door; then there was "Horse's Ass." Our activities ranged from standing around doing nothing to playing baseball, making tree houses, baking potatoes in a cardboard playhouse, and deliberately intruding on the territory of the 30th Street Gang, which almost always resulted in a running fight.

We also challenged other street gangs, such as the Bangor Street and the 31st Street gangs. We looked forward to these confrontations. If a fight broke out, we fought with rocks, fists, and coke bottles, but never with knives or firearms. I must admit I had very good speed and was also very adept at jumping fences!

On one occasion, we ventured about six blocks north and were chased home by the Warren Avenue Gang, which was all-black. Interestingly, the only other contact I had with blacks occurred on Sunday mornings when we went to Scott Methodist Episcopal Church at St. Antoine and Kirby Streets. Both the church and street are long gone, paved over by the urban renewal project that became I-75. Scott Church was a large wooden structure sitting right on the sidewalk. Dad sang in the choir. As a three- or four-year-old, I remember following him up the wooden stairs, past the wainscoted panels, and up into the choir loft. Scott Church was the social and religious center of our lives. At that time, young people's organizations like the Boy Scouts and the Boy's Clubs drew the color line. There was a Boy's Club only eight blocks from my home, but I was not allowed inside. Detroit had one YMCA exclusively for blacks and another one that allowed us to use its facilities, but both were located in the ghetto on the lower east side of the city.

We kids knew all the police who cruised our neighborhood in open four-door roadsters, which we called The Big Four. We would shoot craps on the corner of 28th and Jackson, furtively watching for cops, and, when sighted, we would grab the dice and money and run like hell! Sometimes the cops won, and they would threaten us. They would usually give us back our dice, but never the money! Despite all the trouble we caused, I was never manhandled by the police, who were always white. I had the strange feeling that if I had been anywhere else than forty feet from my front door and a known member of the community and the gang, things might have been different.

I also knew I would not have been so fortunate if something like this had happened in the South. Every summer we traveled to Atlanta to visit my grandfather, and this one time, when I was maybe twelve or thirteen, my grandfather sent me to the corner store. I went in and announced, "I want a nickel's worth of bologna and five cents worth of grits." The indignant owner angrily said, "What did you say, boy?" When I repeated my order, he said, "Don't you know how to speak to me, boy?" I told him, "Hell, no." Fortunately, my grandfather was "the Methodist minister" for black Atlanta so there were no repercussions for him, although he immediately shipped me home to Detroit because I had been so disrespectful.

When I was in fourth or fifth grade I began skipping school and walking some three miles to a small airfield on the corner of Ford Road and Wyoming. I would hang around, doing odd jobs and helping the mechanics work on planes. I also got my first ride in a bi-winged plane that I believe was a Waco. If my mother had known this, she would have killed me.

When I was about eleven, something happened that made me realize I wanted to stay in school. I had become totally uninvolved with my schoolwork because I was bored and unchallenged. Then, one day, my father forgot his lunch, and I had to take it to him at the Detroit Lubricator Company. The walk to the foundry, which was located on Marquette and Trumble Streets, was only a couple of miles, but it was summer and the weather was sticky and hot, probably in the nineties. As I walked into the factory, I was curious about the owner, Eliza McCoy, whom my father had once described as "a Negro man who walks around the plant with an air and is respected wherever he goes." Much later, I learned that Elijah McCoy had been born to fugitive slaves in Canada in the 1840s. He had studied mechanical engineering in Scotland before settling near Ypsilanti, Michigan, after the Civil War. In 1872, he invented an automatic oiler for the wheels and axles of steam engines. When competitors came up with their own inferior versions, train engineers demanded "The Real McCoy." McCoy subsequently moved to Detroit where he opened up the factory where my father worked. When he died in the late 1920s, he held more than forty patents on various mechanical devices.

Of course, I didn't know any of this on that hot summer day, and I certainly

did not see Mr. McCoy when I walked into his factory and asked one of his workers where I could find my father. "Oh, yeah," he said, "Jeff's back in the foundry."

When I reached the foundry, the stifling heat, humidity, and odor hit me in the face, and I almost passed out. My dad was stripped to the waist, sweating like a hog, holding one end of a ladle, with another man on the other end. My dad weighed about 145 pounds, but he was all muscle. The two of them were pouring molten aluminum into sand castings to make carburetors. Seeing my father slaving under those conditions made me swear to myself, "God, if you let me get out of here, I'll never go into a foundry again the rest of my life."

Foundries at that time had no showers or locker rooms for changing clothes. My father had to travel on the streetcar, summer or winter, out of that foundry into the cold or heat. He went through at least four bouts with pneumonia, and the last one finished him. He died in 1954 due to complications of silicosis and pneumonia. X-rays showed that his lungs looked like the black branches of a tree. He was seventy-four.

Strangely enough, I grew up feeling isolated from my two siblings. Emma was five years younger than I, and Clarence was nine years my junior; consequently, growing up we had little in common. While I was out running the streets, Emma was inside with my mother, doing "girls'" work. She entered Clark in September of the year I graduated. She married in 1950 and that same year I finally realized I also had a brother when he began babysitting my daughter, Alexis Louise. Later, we became fishing buddies, and, over the years, all three of us grew very close.

My seventh and eighth grades were spent at Condon Intermediate School at West Grand Boulevard and Buchanan. I transferred to Munger Intermediate for ninth grade in order to take the college preparatory course, which included Latin and college algebra. My determined mother had to have a confrontation with the principal of Condon to expedite this change. Munger Intermediate was located on Martin and McGraw Streets, next to Chadsey High School, which I also attended.

When I was in ninth grade at Munger, I experienced an incident that really angered me. I don't remember the exact language, but my English teacher, a Mrs. Stellberger, made a covertly racist remark that I took personally. In retaliation, I called her a "left-handed shit-grabber." My mother and I had to attend a command conference with the teacher, the counselor, and the principal in order to keep me in school. When the incident was reconstructed, an audible silence came over the room. Mrs. Stellberger and I met again in 1958. She was in the Detroit Federation of Teachers Building stuffing envelopes for the union when I walked in. She looked at me across the table and exclaimed, "Alexander Jefferson! What are you doing here?" I guess it was no surprise that she remembered me.

I had weaned myself away from the 28th Street Gang by the time I began Chadsey High School. Simply put, we were going in different directions. I knew I was going on to college, but my Polish friends and their parents considered finishing high school and going to work in a factory to be the epitome of success.

My years at Chadsey were uneventful except for the intensity of my interest in chemistry and biology and the hours spent in the laboratories. I took great pleasure in drawing the specimens we studied in biology, especially the entrails of a dissected frog. As for the rest of my classes, I passively endured them, satisfied just to receive passing grades. I remember many of these courses were simply too easy and I became bored. So I entertained myself designing and drawing airplanes, multifaceted constellations, and all kinds of ships and cars. I do not

straight through to Atlanta. It was about eight hundred miles, and we'd make it in something less than twenty-four hours. Uncle Norman knew where we could stop to buy gasoline and find a bathroom.

So when I set out on my own, I knew exactly what to do. I had enough money to buy gas, sufficient chicken to snack on, and that was pretty much it. I remember between Lexington and Chattanooga following a Greyhound bus around those dangerous mountain curves on old, two-lane US 25. But Lizzie and I navigated those roads, and we arrived in Atlanta with no problems.

I moved into Grandfather White's house on the south side of Atlanta, just two blocks from Clark College. Grandfather was then the pastor emeritus of the South Atlanta Methodist Church. He was in his late eighties or early nineties and almost blind, but he was still performing hard physical labor. My grandfather owned eight or nine shotgun houses that he rented out, and it was a full-time job to keep them in repair. I remember being with him on a two-story roof and him saying, "Alex, give me a nail! Now, show me where it goes?" I'd place his hand on the spot; he'd feel it with his finger, place the nail, and pound it in. He did this while sitting on the edge of the roof, with his feet hanging over the edge, and me hanging onto the top of the ladder, trying to keep him from slipping off.

Helping him, I learned how to mix red mud, cement, and lime to make plaster for walls. I also learned how to repair toilets with used plumbing materials, patch roofs with makeshift paper and cardboard, mix concrete with sand, gravel, lime, and a little cement, and fix rotting windows and porches. You name it, Grandpa could repair it. At the time, I weighed 110 pounds dripping wet, and when we used a big crosscut saw to cut up crossties for the fireplace, I can still hear him yelling, "Pull that saw, boy! Don't push it!"

I loved eating breakfast with my grandfather because it was so different from the shredded wheat and cold milk I was used to at home. I would wake up to the wonderful aroma of grits, gravy, biscuits, and pork chops. And if I needed something to eat later in the day, I could stop at the corner drug store and buy a pig-ear sandwich for a nickel. A boiled pig's ear slapped between a couple of slices of bread and covered with lots of mustard and relish was simply delicious. I'd top that off with a Coke that was much stronger than anything we drink today. Coca-Cola really was Coca-Cola back in those days.

I have many fond memories of South Atlanta during my college years. First, there was the wonderful relationship I had with Lizzie. We drove around together for five years, interrupted only by the nine months when I was undergoing my pilot training at Tuskegee Army Air Field. We spent three years on the old campus at Clark and one at the new campus, which was located in the inner city across from Morehouse College. Owning a car made me a Big Man on Campus. A couple of guys rode with me every day to the new campus, and each gave me a nickel for gas. Lizzie and I were also on the cheerleading squad at Clark. I was too light to play football and too short for basketball, but we cheerleaders had great fun climbing in Lizzie and following the teams to the away games.

I was always very conscious of the fact I was a "Northern Negro." Because of this and my dark complexion and lack of involvement in politically active campus organizations, I was not accepted into the socially exclusive Alpha Phi Alpha fraternity, which took great pride that its members were "light, bright, and damn near white."

I did just fine without fraternity life because I spent most of my time at Clark in the labs or on dates. Lizzie and I often drove our ladies into the city or the surrounding countryside; in fact, I seem to recall two or three very nice, secluded lovers' lanes!

Clark's move to its new campus in the center of Atlanta greatly affected student life. Everything seemed in turmoil. New buildings were going up everywhere, traffic was heavy, and the pace of life was more hectic. We Clark males entered into gentlemanly competition for our co-eds with our counterparts at Morehouse, which was an all-male school. And the males from both schools competed for the girls of Spellman, which was a girls' school just down the street. Atlanta University was no threat because its graduate students were older and much more serious. God, did we have fun!

I majored in chemistry and biology and minored in physics and math. I was badgered but sustained by Professor Brooks, a light-skinned Jamaican. His wife, Stella Brooks, was head of the English Department and a virtual dictator. For thirty years, she remained the bulwark of the English departments at Clark College and Atlanta University. I flunked her English course because, I now realize, I resented her autocratic attitude. But ironically, ten years later, I grew to respect, revere, and embrace her holy trinity of grammar, rhetoric, and punctuality, upon which she stood and from which she refused to be moved.

I was in the Philharmonic Society and the Clark Choir, led by the one and only J. DeKoven Killingsworth, a left-handed, cockeyed, strawberry-splotched, red-haired, straight-fingered musical genius. You could never tell in which direction he was looking. Between long hours in the chemistry, biology, and physics labs and my many soirees with Lizzie around Atlanta and its surrounding countryside, I often barely made rehearsals on time. We frequently went on tour, performing in black churches in such fascinating cities as Washington, Philadelphia, Cleveland, Chicago, St Louis, and Memphis. We traveled by bus, and the girls were very well chaperoned. I sang first bass in the male quartet, and during every concert the audience always requested us to sing two or three spirituals.

Life on the original Clark College campus was a wonderful experience. It was situated in the midst of a hundred acres of serene woods. This isolation meant we didn't come in contact with racism unless, of course, we went off campus, where everything was segregated, even the water fountains. We were forced to sit at the back of buses and streetcars, but in the front car of trains, right behind the soot and steam of the engines. The campus of Georgia Tech was off-limits to persons of color, and we were not allowed to try on clothes at Riches Department Store in downtown Atlanta. We could go to the movie theaters, but we had to sit in the balcony. The theater we most frequented in Atlanta was the Fox. We bought our tickets at the front box office, but then had to walk around to the side of the building and climb a long steel stairway to the balcony.

Even the parks were segregated. We played our homecoming football game with archrival Morris Brown College at Ponce de Leon Park. Normally, this park was off-limits to us, but for this auspicious annual event, the city allowed us to use it. The city even ran streetcars to the campus gate. The students would board and ride up Capital Avenue, through downtown Atlanta, and then out to Ponce de Leon Park for our grand celebration. All of black Atlanta would turn out. Of course, I loaded up Lizzie with the female cheerleaders, and we escorted the streetcars and other vehicles with great fanfare. I can still see that 1932 roadster, with its big balloon tires and wire spokes, its rumble seat filled with those cute cheerleaders, honking its way to Ponce de Leon Park for the big game. Except for the driver, it was a reputed fact that Lizzie never carried a "hard leg," which refers to the male of the species. Atlanta was then a dry city, so we also carried with us our sweet syrupy Southern Comfort, mixed in coke bottles, and a good time was had by all!

This marvelously carefree undergraduate life ended for me at 10:30 on the morning of June 2, 1942, when my class became the first to graduate from the new campus. After the formal ceremony, there was no great celebration. I recall no graduation pictures, dances, or parties. It was simply time to leave, so I packed up Lizzie and headed home to Detroit.

3 The Making of a Tuskegee Airman

It was June 1942, there was a war on, and I was back home in Detroit after my graduation from Clark. I knew I was going to be drafted, but I had high hopes I would be able to join the Army Air Corps. Actually, blacks had been fighting for the right to join the Air Corps since World War I. Finally, on April 3, 1939, Public Law 18 called for an expansion of the Air Corps, including the authorization of programs in black colleges to train African Americans for Air Corps support services. Then, on January 16, 1941, the War Department contracted with Tuskegee Institute to train black pilots for what would become the 99th Fighter Squadron. This was during my junior year at Clark, so when recruiters came on campus to sign up volunteers, I immediately wrote home asking permission to join. Although I was then old enough to sign up without parental permission, my dad very emphatically said, "Hell no! If you were meant to fly, you would've been born with wings. Now, finish college!" It was the first time I had ever heard the old man swear. As a dutiful son, I complied.

I had always wanted to fly, and my hobby of building model airplanes had continued even during my college days. After Pearl Harbor, I knew that if I were drafted, I would end up as a buck private earning $21 a month in a segregated quartermaster company, forced to perform heavy, nasty, dirty work. But the life of a flying cadet meant $75 a month and a fancy uniform that was sure to attract beautiful women. After nine months, my pay would increase to $150 a month, plus $75 flying pay. I would also have my wings, and, with any luck, even more lovely ladies!

After I returned to Detroit, I went down to the Federal Building and passed the written examination for the Army Air Corps with flying colors, but I flunked the physical. I weighed 116½ pounds and the minimum was 117. I was told to go downstairs, drink some water, and eat a couple of bananas. When I returned, I got on the scales and just made it. On September 23, 1942, I was sworn into the Army Reserves. I immediately volunteered for flight training but was told to return home and wait for a position to open up. When I asked when this would be, I was told not to worry about it. I wasn't sure I would ever be called, but at least being in the reserves kept me from being drafted. At the time, I didn't understand what was going on, but I later learned there was a rigid quota restricting how many blacks could be inducted each month into the training program at Tuskegee.

Disappointed, I returned to my old 28th Street neighborhood, only to find that it had greatly changed because of the war. Many of my old friends were already in the armed services. I didn't want just to sit around, so I got a job in a small steel-treating plant on East Six Mile. I worked as an analytical chemist, running carbon analysis tests on the steel that came out of the furnaces. Surprisingly, that job paid me twice as much as my father was then making as a laborer.

I held that job from about June 15 until the middle of September 1942, when I had an unexpected opportunity to begin graduate school. I've already mentioned Mrs. Clark, who lived across the street from us. Her grandson, Martin Jenkins, who was ten or fifteen years older than I, was then on the faculty of Howard University in Washington, D.C. When he came to Detroit that summer for a visit, we talked about graduate school. Through his efforts I was accepted at Howard as a graduate student in the Chemistry Department. Martin Jenkins would later become president of Morgan State University in Baltimore.

I had long had an interest in chemistry. My mother had always insisted that I read, and she encouraged me to go to the local library, where, after spending countless hours thumbing through scientific textbooks and pamphlets, I decided I wanted to become a research chemist. I always knew I had the intellectual ability to accomplish whatever I wished, and if any doubts ever crept into my mind, the firm hand of my mother quickly dispelled them.

So, once again, I drove Lizzie off to school. In Washington, I shared a basement apartment on Sixth Street with a guy named Cotton, right across the street from the chemistry building. To help defray my expenses, I taught a freshman class in organic chemistry. My life centered almost exclusively on that chemistry building. I have no memory of any other campus activities, not even of entering any other buildings on campus, except the library. The one professor who stands out in my mind was Dr. Sherashefsky, who had just returned from doing secret research for the government and had become very ill. Only later did I learn that his research dealt with the effects of radiation.

I rarely wandered off campus, and I never went downtown to visit the museums or other tourist attractions because wartime Washington was still a very racist city and completely segregated. The one section of the city I could and did occasionally visit was bordered by Seventh Street, U Street, and Florida Avenue, located five or six blocks south of Howard University. On these fascinating and vibrant streets I could come alive. I greatly enjoyed listening to the moving gospel music of the storefront churches on Seventh Street, performed with tambourines, guitars, organs, and drums, and I found the jazz and blues played at the Baptist church equally compelling.

The cultural center for black Washington, however, was the Howard Theater, where every Friday night, when the venue changed, the first ten rows were filled with Howard University students. All the great vaudeville stars and acts from the Chitlin Circuit played the Howard Theater. I remember seeing Cab Calloway, Fats Waller, Duke Ellington, Count Basie, Chick Webb, Ella Fitzgerald, Billy Eckstein, Jackson & Patterson, and "Here Come Da Judge" Peg Leg Bates.

I never finished my first year at Howard because I received my orders to begin my flight training in April 1943. The notice to report to the Tuskegee Army Air Field (TAAF) went to Detroit, and my family immediately notified me. I was so excited about having my class date that I immediately notified the Chemistry Department I was leaving school, and then drove Lizzie home to Detroit.

Once again Lizzie went up on blocks in the barn, and I got ready to head south. When the C&O train left from the old train station on Michigan Avenue and 14th Street, I rode coach. In Cincinnati, however, I transferred to the Louisville and Nashville Line, which meant all blacks had to move to the first car behind the coal burning steam engine. The South's discriminatory travel arrangements were not new to me, but it was still hard to endure the soot and hard seats. There were also no food or lavatory facilities for blacks, and the odor of urine was disgusting. But this was the way black soldiers went to war, at least in the South.

In Atlanta, I again changed trains, and boarded one heading for Montgomery, Alabama. I remember the porter calling out such stops as Fairburn, LaGrange, and West Point, Georgia and then Opelika, Auburn and finally Chehaw, Alabama, where nine or ten of us future cadets got off.

It was ten o'clock at night, and we could see nothing except a small building about a hundred yards away. As we walked toward it, we could make out the word "Chehaw" on the end. There was nothing else, no town, nothing. We had no idea what we were supposed to do, so we just stood there. Finally, a 6 × 6

Chehaw Train Station, Alabama. Alexander Jefferson (l.) with Chauncey E. Spencer, who promoted the Civilian Pilot Training Program for blacks, and Wardell Polk, a member of the 477th Bomber Group, who was arrested for protesting discriminatory policies in 1945.

army truck rolled up and the driver told us to get in. At precisely eleven o'clock at night on April 13, 1943, we arrived at the Tuskegee Army Air Field to begin our training.

We cadets were all college graduates and highly motivated and aggressive. I look back now and realize to be black then and survive, you had to be that way. I think there were ninety of us who started in Class 44-A, so called because we were supposed to graduate in January 1944. By the end of our nine months of training, only twenty-five of us had survived. Some were eliminated for flying inadequacies and some for nonmilitary reasons. Years later, through the Freedom of Information Act, we discovered there had been a quota for how many blacks were allowed to graduate. The phrase used to wash guys out was "eliminated while passing for the convenience of the government."

The night before graduation all of us who had made it that far went to sleep, fully expecting to pin on our wings the next day. The next morning, however, we discovered that three or four members of our class had been pulled out and told they were not going to graduate. Some of them had even purchased their uniforms and invited their parents and sweethearts to come to graduation. It was a loss of their manhood, and it caused them a lot of psychological stress; in fact, some of them are still psychologically wounded because they were washed out. I know some of these guys could fly better than I could, and they were certainly better soldiers. Hell, I was a damned civilian, not a soldier.

The training itself was very challenging and very hectic. The specific details remain a blur, as we worked our way through the stages of preflight, primary, basic, and advanced training. I do remember being harassed by the upperclassmen. We were the "Dummies," which meant we were supposed to be hazed. There was constant deep knee bending, duck walking, and sitting on an imaginary little red stool with your back braced against the wall, arms across your chest, and alternately kicking your feet out and back. We'd also be rousted in the middle of the night by upperclassmen, just in from night flying, who took great delight in ordering us to do our best imitation of a plane, "flying" up and down the hall with our arms outstretched.

I never took the hazing personally. I knew it was a way to weed out those who could not stand up under adverse stress or take direct and rigorous commands. There was no physical contact, just psychological abuse, which many men could not handle.

Air Cadet Alexander Jefferson.

The one pleasant interlude was a glorious day between preflight and primary training when I returned to Atlanta and strutted through campus and my other old haunts, showing off the splendor of my new uniform. When I visited my old chemistry and biology labs, the freshmen and even the professors looked at me in awe.

On July 1, 1943, we completed our preflight training and moved on to primary, which was conducted on the campus of Tuskegee Institute. Our preflight training had consisted of three months of ground and flight training, which had been commercially farmed out to Tuskegee Institute. The ground and flight instructors were black civilians. Chief Charles Alfred Anderson, who a few years earlier had taken Mrs. Eleanor Roosevelt for a plane ride to convince her that blacks could fly, was the supervisor of the flight instructors. In contrast, all instructors at the Tuskegee Army Air Field, where we took our basic and advanced training, were white regular army personnel.

I want to say something about Colonel Noel F. Parrish, the white, Southern-born commander of the Tuskegee Army Air Field when I went through training. In December 1942, he had replaced Colonel Frederick Kimble, the first Tuskegee commander, who was much more interested in maintaining total segregation on base—including ordering white officers not to fraternize with their black cadets—than he was in training future pilots. Parrish himself was not a crusader for civil rights, but, unlike Kimble, he was determined that we should succeed. His father had been an itinerant minister in Kentucky, Georgia, and Alabama. Colonel Parrish had attended Rice Institute in Texas for a couple of years before enlisting. He eventually earned his commission and became a flight instructor in the Army Air Corps. His standards for us were every bit as high as for the white pilots he had previously trained. He insisted that anything less would get us killed, and he was quite willing to wash out anyone who did not perform up to his high expectations. Above all, he tried to stand up for us when many of his superiors wanted us to fail.

For our primary training we were assigned rooms in the basement of a dormitory just inside the campus gate. My class and class 43-J went through primary at the same time. My class included four other cadets from Michigan: Robert Cain, Leon Duncan Coleman, and Wardell Polk, all from Detroit, and Charles Walker from Jackson. We flew in the morning and attended classes in the afternoon. The other class did just the opposite. Classes were held in the building next to the dormitory in which we were staying. We ate in the mess hall across the square. I do not recall visiting any other buildings on campus because we were far too busy.

We did our early flying at Moten Field, which was five or six miles from the Tuskegee campus. It was a dirt field with a couple of large hangers, one of which had a tall parachute-training tower alongside it. For our primary training, we flew the PT-17 Stearman, a tandem two-seater with two fabric-covered wings and an open cockpit. My instructor was Perry Young, a black civilian pilot from the Coffee School of Aeronautics, a private flight school at Harlem Airport on the south side of Chicago, where Cornelius R. Coffey and Willa Brown had first promoted aviation in the black community in the 1930s and '40s.

I was the first in my class to solo, doing so after eight hours. Then I ground looped, which meant I landed too high, and when the wheels touched down, the plane veered off to the right and the wing dragged the ground. This happened about six days before our class was scheduled to leave for basic training, but I passed my final check ride, and, with the other survivors, returned to the

Tuskegee Army Air Field for basic, where we flew the Vultee BT-13, which we called the "Vibrator."

Each class lost guys to accidents. I think we lost two men out of our class. We knew this happened in every class, but, as individuals, we figured it always happened to somebody else. We were young, and we considered ourselves invincible. I remember during primary training at Moten Field one morning a B-26 came smoking in for a landing. All hell broke loose! The pilot had lost an engine on takeoff from TAAF about ten miles away, and Moten Field was the closest field he could see. They had to truck the plane out because it was impossible to fly, but fortunately no one was hurt.

Another unforgettable sight was seeing and hearing a P-40 go straight in from high altitude. It's very eerie to hear the piercing whine of a plane as it increases in speed, going straight in. The date was July 9, 1943, and Lieutenant Oscar Kenny lost his life.

After we moved from primary at Moten to TAAF for basic and then advanced training, there was still some hazing from upper classmen, but not nearly as much because we were now becoming upperclassmen, with dummies below us whom we were supposed to help train. After all, our future life in combat might very well depend on them.

Advanced training was fascinating. Night cross-country trips were especially challenging. Once again, I ground looped, this time in the BT-13, because I was careless and inattentive. My airspeed dropped below stall, and the plane fell in from twenty feet and bounced over on a wing. Nevertheless, I again passed my final check ride, this time with Gabe Hawkins, who was called Old Scar Face because of the scars he incurred when his face smashed into the instrument panel during a crash landing.

Graduation was an exciting day. My mother came down from Detroit, and my grandfather came from Atlanta, along with my sister, Emma, and our cousin, Gwendolyn, both of whom were attending Clark College. I was standing tall, dressed smartly in my "pinks and greens," with my new wings proudly attached to my chest. It was an exhilarating experience for the twenty-two of us who graduated on January 7, 1944, as second lieutenants. There were also three regular army infantry officers who had joined our class, Fred Parker, Charles Hunter and Leon Turner, and they too received their wings.

After graduation, I enjoyed a ten-day leave in Washington, D.C. I went to the

Graduation day for newly commissioned Lt. Alexander Jefferson, January 7, 1944. From left: Emma Jefferson, sister; Henry White, grandfather; Jefferson; Jane Jefferson, mother; Gwendolyn Coffee, cousin.

city with Arthur Wilburn, who was in my class at Tuskegee and whose sister, Margo, I had met at graduation. During my ten days in Washington, Margo and I developed quite a relationship. She was about five-foot-two, 110 pounds, with shoulder-length brown hair, green eyes, and a very smooth and fair complexion. My, my, my, such memories! In fact, I named the plane I flew in combat "Margo." We exchanged letters while I was overseas, at least until I became a POW. I continued to write her but heard nothing more from her. When I returned to the States after the war, I discovered that some of my good buddies had taken care of Margo, and I never saw her again.

After my furlough in Washington, I returned to the Tuskegee Army Air Field for another several weeks to fly P-40s. These planes, with the angry tiger teeth emblazoned on their cowling, had returned from Burma and were really beat up. Nevertheless, it was a great thrill to hear the whine of that Allison engine and feel the torque of the prop on take off. Taxiing down the runway, you'd hear the popping and spitting of the engine because the magnetos didn't quite match the valve closings, and you'd get a lump in your throat because the nose sat so high you had to zigzag in order to see where you were going.

tight circle, called a luftberry, with four or five other P-39s around the Maccabees Building, in midtown Detroit: roaring 1500-horsepower single engines, eleven-foot props, flames shooting out of the open exhaust side stacks, kicking hard right rudder, throttles wide open in order to maintain altitude, which we figured to be about 200 feet, and speed, which was barely 150 mph! From there we went streaming at treetop height over the Trowbridge and Harmon neighborhood, which was where the girls we were trying to impress lived. When we returned to base, we expected to catch hell and be reprimanded, but when interrogated, we, of course, were prepared to deny everything on a stack of Bibles.

Our instructors were First Lieutenants Charles Dryden and Spann Watson, along with another pilot whose name I cannot recall, who had all flown in combat in 1943 in North Africa with the all-black 99th Fighter Squadron. They were now assigned to our 553rd Fighter Replacement Squadron, along with the white instructors, to train replacement pilots for the 332nd Fighter and the 477th Bomber Groups.

I'll never forget when Dryden, Watson, and this other black instructor plotted a low-level, cross-Michigan navigation flight to train us to fly on the deck, at treetop height, to avoid enemy fire. We first flew north to the Thumb area around Bad Axe, then west to Mt. Pleasant, south across Adrian and Monroe, and then back up the Detroit River to Lake St. Clair and Selfridge Field. Dryden told us, "There will be an instructor every ten to fifteen miles checking you out. We do not want to see anyone above fifty feet, and we mean no one!"

We had a ball. We dropped our planes down over the trees onto level fields and blew farmers off their tractors. The first plane through a farmyard blew chickens into the air, and the second and third plane would have chicken feathers and entrails clinging to their radiators. We had clothes lines wrapped around our props and grass stains on the tips. We played follow the leader coming up the Detroit River from Monroe. We were so low over the river that the eleven-foot prop threw up a spray like a rooster tail. I don't know how many of us flew under the Ambassador Bridge, but I know I did. What fun!

Gunnery practice with our 37 mm cannons on Lake Huron firing at a large 50-foot target floating on the water was tough. Every time you fired the cannon, you lost 5–7 mph of airspeed. Clarence "Red" Driver, trying to get too close to get a good score, was too low when he fired, and the shell hit the water and threw up a tall plume. His plane hit it, shuddered, and almost stalled, and the tail dragged the water before the prop pulled the plane out of the water. When he landed, the leading edge of the wing had been beaten back three to four inches where the water had hit it. The plane was "class 26" or "red-lined," which meant it was removed from flying status.

We stayed at Selfridge until May 10, 1944, when we were forced to leave because we attempted to integrate the officers' club in Luftberry Hall. Colonel Robert Selway Jr. had been the commanding officer of the 332nd Fighter Group until it left Selfridge to go to Italy in January 1944, and he continued to command the 477th Bomber Group, which remained at Selfridge. He was a West Point graduate who was determined to make life as miserable as possible for black airmen. He was convinced that African Americans were inferior and lacked the necessary skills to be combat pilots. He also believed they should never be put in supervisory positions. Agreeing with his racist policies were Lieutenant Colonel Charles A. Gayle, who was the commanding officer of our 553rd Replacement Squadron, Colonel William L. Boyd, the base commander, and Major General Frank O'Driscoll Hunter of the 1st Air Force, all of whom were willing to jeopardize our training and the war effort in order to maintain separate and second-class status for every African American under their command. Their policies also violated Army Regulation 210-10, which mandated that officers' clubs and other social organizations offer "all officers on duty at the post the right to full membership, either permanent or temporary."

Matters came to a head when we raised grievances about being denied admittance to the officers' club in Luftberry Hall. The problem was all black officers were classified on the morning report as "transient personnel," even though Dryden and Watson had been there for two months or longer. Upon arrival, all white officers were immediately classified as permanent, and only permanent personnel had officers' club privileges. To compound the indignity, we had to pay our monthly six dollars officers' dues just like everybody else. When we complained to the club officer, who was, of course, white, he ordered the installation of a wooden bar in a tiny room in the barracks and told us that would be our officers' club. We refused to accept this, so every day we tried to enter the white officers' club, and every day we were turned away. The NAACP, the Urban League, and the *Michigan Chronicle*, which was a black newspaper, began pressuring the authorities to break down these barriers.

We were having gunnery practice over Lake Huron when our radios blared,

"All officers report to the post theater, as you are, on the double!" That meant everyone, black and white, so we wheeled around, flew back to the base, and walked into the post theater still clad in our flying uniforms. There were fifteen members of my Tuskegee class and approximately twenty-five or thirty other black officers on base who were ground and support personnel. I don't know how many white officers there were, but we all went inside trying to figure out what was going on. Someone yelled, "Ten-hut!" We popped to, and down the aisle came General O. D. Hunter, who had flown in for the meeting. Hunter then shouted, "At ease, gentlemen." We sat down. He rambled on for about five or ten minutes about problems at Selfridge, and then he said, and I remember his words exactly, "Gentlemen, this is my airfield. As long as I am in command, there will be no socialization between white and colored officers." He paused and then asked, "Are there any questions? If there are, I will deal with that man personally." Hell, we were second lieutenants, at the bottom of the officer ladder. What could we say? We sat there in shock and just looked at each other. Then somebody yelled, "Ten-hut!" and he walked out.

That was a Thursday. We were immediately confined to the post. The gates were locked, and our telephones were disconnected, so there was no way we could communicate with the outside world. In truth, we were under post arrest! On Saturday morning a train backed into Selfridge, and all officers and enlisted personnel of the 553rd were loaded and locked in with just our bags. No one told us where we were going. We first went north to Port Huron, then across to Sarnia, Canada, and on to Niagara Falls, from where the train headed south. To this day, we have never seen the PCS Orders (Permanent Change of Station Orders) that sent us from Selfridge Army Air Base to Walterboro Army Air Base in South Carolina.

Although I didn't know the details at the time, the all-black 477th Bomber Group, which had likewise been preparing for combat, was also expelled from Selfridge. They were first sent to Godman Field, just outside of Fort Knox, Kentucky, and then, several months later, transferred to Freeman Field, Indiana, about sixty miles south of Indianapolis. They were still under the command of Colonel Selway, whose discriminatory policies once again led to trouble. On April 1, 1945, he posted an order restricting certain buildings to whites only. When several groups of black officers attempted to integrate the whites-only officers club, he had them arrested. On April 9, Colonel Selway, with the approval of General Hunter, posted Regulation 85-2, which mandated the strict segregation of all base facilities. He then ordered all officers, black and white, to affirm and sign that they had read, understood, and accepted the conditions of Regulation 85-2. When 101 black officers, including future mayor of Detroit Coleman Young, who was one of the leaders, refused, the result was the so-called "Freeman Field Mutiny." All were arrested. Some were court-martialed, and others received letters of reprimand. Army Chief of Staff General George C. Marshall and Chief of Air Staff General Barney Giles, fearing political repercussions, intervened and ordered the men released; however, not until 1995 were these men fully exonerated and their records expunged of all charges. In June 1945 Colonel Selway was finally relieved of his command of the 477th Bomber Group and replaced by Colonel Benjamin O. Davis Jr., but by this time it was too late for these men and they never saw combat.

Walterboro Army Air Base was some forty-five miles west of Charleston. It was one of a string of bases built along the Atlantic seaboard to defend against a possible invasion. It was another segregated base—and this time in a segregated state. When our train backed onto the base, we were greeted by white soldiers in full battle dress. There they stood, one every thirty feet along both sides of the train, with rifles and bayonets at the ready. We found out later they had been told to prepare for "a train full of rowdy niggers who have just rioted at Selfridge Field." There we were, in our Class A uniforms, trying to look our best. After we chatted with these soldiers about how things were in Walterboro, they quietly disappeared.

You have to understand that all this reflected the reality of the times. We were still second-class citizens, especially in the South. The unspoken rule in the military then was if you went counter to the local or state laws, no one would back you up. You were left on your own. We knew this. It was all part of coping, and we knew we had to deal with it. We tested the system, as best we could. It was a constant struggle, but our willingness to challenge the system helped us survive.

We were at Walterboro for only a few weeks, but again we tried to assert ourselves by integrating the post theater. There was a rope down the center of the theater to separate white and black soldiers. One night somebody cut the rope, after which the officer of the day closed the theater.

We were still flying the P-39 Airocobras at Walterboro when our old instructor from Selfridge, Charles Dryden, led three of us on an orientation and exploratory flight around the field and the surrounding countryside. I was on his right wing as number two; Robert Oneal was on his left at number three, with Frederick McIver next to him as number four. We flew over the swamps of South Carolina, the islands off the coast, and every little town within twenty-five or thirty miles. It was a Sunday morning, and, returning to base, Dryden proceeded to circle a Walterboro church at about a hundred feet. We were separated from each other by maybe twenty feet. Then we flew right down the main street of Walterboro. It was great fun, and it allowed us to express our contempt for all the abuse and racism we had suffered. We fully expected to catch hell after landing, but, strangely enough, no one said anything, although the men in the tower certainly knew what we had done.

Another memory of Walterboro was wearing full jungle survival gear in case of engine failure on takeoff, because there were all kinds of alligators and snakes in the swamp at the end of the runway.

On May 26, 1944, our group of fifteen replacement pilots received orders to get on a train in Walterboro to travel to Camp Patrick Henry, Virginia, where we were going to board a ship for North Africa. We had these vouchers we were supposed to exchange in the tiny, ten-by-ten-foot Walterboro Railroad Station for tickets that would entitle us to Pullman accommodations. The ticket clerk ordered us to go around to the back of the ticket office, but we refused, and things got nasty. We picked up our Thompson submachine guns, for which we were not supposed to have ammunition. Then a large group of angry white civilians armed with shotguns showed up, yelling and screaming that they were going to burn some niggers. We responded by ramming in our ammunition clips. All of a sudden everything got very quiet. The train sat there for at least forty-five minutes before the base colonel came screeching up in his staff car, accompanied by several trucks filled with white soldiers. The colonel tried to get us to give up our weapons, but we refused. Finally, the engineer said, "Get on board, fellas." We did, but we still didn't have our tickets.

I will never forget that train ride to Camp Patrick Henry, because we were absolutely sure when we arrived we would be met by armed guards, arrested, and faced court-martial. But nothing happened. We were assigned to barracks, along with our weapons, and settled in to await shipment overseas.

4 Combat

The fifteen of us who graduated in Tuskegee Class 44-A were classified as replacement pilots for the 332nd Fighter Group. On June 3, 1944, we boarded a troopship bound for North Africa. Ironically, we black pilots were the only male officers who had our cabins above deck. There were thousands of enlisted personnel below deck, and their officers were with them. A contingency of twenty white nurses also had their cabins topside, right across the corridor from us. We visited, sunbathed, and ate together, and a good time was had by all.

The ship ran a solo, high-speed, zigzag course across the Atlantic. The captain said that we were doing up to thirty knots. Every ten minutes or so he would order the ship to change course about fifteen degrees, I assume to make us a more difficult target for German submarines. After an uneventful and very pleasant seven days, we landed in Oran, on the northeast coast of Algeria, on June 8, 1944.

After just a few days in Oran, Algeria, the fifteen of us, plus hundreds of regular troops, shipped out to Naples on an Indian tramp steamer. I have no idea why they put us on this Indian ship, but the smell and taste of the curry are still with me. The weather was balmy and sunny, which again made the voyage most enjoyable. When we docked in Naples, an army captain, who was in charge of the port battalion, loudly greeted us: "Hey, where in hell have you guys been? We've been waiting for you for a week." Instead of putting us in the regular barracks, he housed us in an apartment complex, most of whose residents were ladies of the evening.

We didn't realize that we were "distinguished" guests who were being watched by everyone up and down the echelon ladder. I'm not sure why; maybe it was because the 100th, 301st, and the 302nd Squadrons of the 332nd Fighter Group had been stationed at Capodichino Air Base, just outside of Naples, and black officers with wings always made white officers nervous. We only stayed in Naples three or four days, but we did have a wonderful time seeing the beautiful churches, buildings, parks, and Herculaneum, the city that Vesuvius had covered but that had later been excavated. We hated to leave, but we had no choice.

The fifteen of us climbed on 6 × 6 army trucks for a nightmare ride to the Ramitelli Air Base, which was located on the other side of the peninsula. We drove on bumpy, two-lane, hazardous dirt roads for several hours before arriving at the shore of the Adriatic Sea early on the morning of June 20, 1944. Just as our trucks were pulling onto the base, we saw planes from the 332nd taking off on what would be their last P-47 combat mission. One of the planes pulled up into a steep climb, shuttered into a stall, fell off on a wing, and went in, erupting in a huge ball of flame. This was our introduction into the world of a combat pilot, but we were almost nonchalant about it because we were sure nothing like this could ever happen to any of us.

The airbase itself consisted of a metal strip runway that had been laid across a wheat field about a quarter of a mile from the Adriatic, just outside the small town of Ramitelli. Next to the runway was a farmhouse that we used as group headquarters. Our 332nd Red-Tail Fighter Group consisted of four squadrons and their designations: the 99th "Subsoil" had white trim tab colors on its rudders and ailerons, the 100th "Counter" black, the 301st "Bubbles" blue, and the 302nd "Doorknob" yellow.

The 52nd Fighter Group, flying P-51 Yellow-Tails, was located about five miles north of us at Madna. The 325th Fighter Group's P-51 Checker-Board Tails were about twenty-five miles east of us along the coast at Lesina. And the 31st Fighter Squadron's P-51 Candy-Stripe-Tails were located some twenty miles south of the 325th at San Severo. These last three were exclusively white squadrons.

Each squadron would put up four flights of four planes, plus two spares. The flights were always designated as Red, White, Blue, and Yellow. Spares were Squadron Spare One and Spare Two. The squadron's lead flight was Red One and its pilot was the squadron leader for that mission. Red Two was his wingman and flew to his right and slightly behind him. Red Three was an element leader and flew to Red One's left and a little farther behind. Red Four flew on Red Three's left and a little behind him.

I was assigned to a tent in the 301st Squadron with William Faulkner, Othell Dickson, and Joseph Elsberry. Our tent, which had a wooden floor made from crates, was about fifteen feet square and, because it was June, we were able to roll up the sides for much needed ventilation. We slept on cots covered with mosquito netting, but we also had DDT, in green-colored spray canisters, which really did a job on the mosquitoes. Our headquarters building was an Italian farmer's stucco-block house. The runway was metal meshing, as were the parking ramps.

We arrived just in time for Ramitelli's transition from P-47s to P-51s. Getting accustomed to the P-51 was very easy. It was a smooth upgrade on the AT-6 and an absolutely outstanding airplane. We flew the B and C models. I flew my first mission after only three hours of transition, but I felt entirely assured and competent, in spite of witnessing a fatal accident involving my tent mate, Othell Dickson. Dickson, who had graduated ahead of me in Class 43K, was a real hotshot, but he was flying the P-51 for the first time. From the flight line, I watched him fly across our tent area at about fifty feet, then pull up into a slow roll, fall out of it, barely recover, and come within ten feet of hitting the ground. This brought all the guys out on the field, wondering who was this fool inviting a court-martial by the 332nd Fighter Group Commander, Colonel Benjamin O. Davis. Dickson then came back around again, and this time, starting at about twenty feet, he pulled up into a near sixty-degree angle and simply fell out the maneuver. He went in upside-down just outside the tent area.

When we tried to recover his charred body, we found only the torso, minus head, feet, and hands, but still sitting in the pilot position and attitude. Dickson had not read the tech orders on the plane or he would have known not to attempt any acrobatics with the fuselage gas tank holding more than half of its eighty-five gallon capacity. When it was too full, it put the center of gravity too far aft, resulting in loss of control when put in the wrong attitude. Again, my personal reaction was not so much emotional as it was practical. I said to myself, "RTDM!" (Read The Damn Manual!)

I have no detailed record of the missions I flew, but I know I flew eighteen without ever missing a scheduled mission until I was shot down on August 12, 1944. We normally flew long-range missions, escorting B-24s and B-17s to their targets over Greece, Bulgaria, Hungary, Poland, Germany, and France, but we also flew strafing missions. I flew mostly as a wingman and did not have my own plane until just before my final mission. When new planes arrived or new engines were installed, the older pilots always had first choice. As a replacement pilot, I had to fly what was left. When I finally did get my own plane, I named her *Margo*, for the young lady I met while on leave in Washington, D.C.

Our missions followed a prescribed routine. We'd awake by any means we could, trying not to disturb our tent mates in case they were not scheduled to fly and wanted to sleep. We'd wash, shave, brush our teeth, and then head for the

THE LUFTGANSTER — IN HIS HEYDAY!

mess tent, where we'd eat some very strange-tasting food that I suspect was flavored by the hundred-octane gas that fueled the stoves. After this unsavory breakfast, we'd return to our tents, put on our flying suits, boots, gloves, chutes, goggles, and watches, grab our cigarettes, and head to the group briefing tent. The briefing officer was usually Colonel Davis, the group commander, or his operations officer, Major Ed Gleed. A huge map of the entire European theater covered the wall. If a red string extended from Ramitelli and a green string from another airfield in Italy came together around the coast of Yugoslavia, we knew it would be an escort mission.

Margo, Alexander Jefferson's combat plane.

Someone would shout, "Attention," and the briefing officer would enter. We would pop to and stand at attention. The briefing officer would respond, "At ease!" and everyone would sit down.

If the briefing officer said, "Gentlemen, today we go to Ploesti," he would be greeted with a resounding "Oh, s——!" If there was only one red string ending in an area occupied by the enemy, it was a strafing mission, which usually also brought expletives from the fighter pilots because this meant being exposed to ground fire from enemy troops. If it was an escort mission, we would also be told whether we would be protecting B-17s or B-24s. We much preferred B-24s because the B-17s were slower, and we had to stay with them longer, which meant we used too much of our precious fuel.

The briefing officer would tell us the type of mission, the mission target, intelligence reports on anticipated ground fire and aerial attacks at the target, and possible partisan support, including what they might be wearing and their identifying armbands or headbands.

For a mission to Ploesti, Romania, the line would angle northeast with a dip marking the place and time where we would pick up the bombers and another dip showing the time and place we would release them and to whom. We would then mark course, altitude, position, and bomber and fighter IDs on pads strapped to our knees.

We would synchronize our watches and receive our engine startup and take-off time, as well as our start-on course time, our estimated rendezvous time and place, and the estimated total mission time. An intelligence officer would then come in and give the latest flak report, informing us which areas to avoid because of heavy concentrations. These reports were invariably wrong, as we almost always encountered the most devastating flak over areas that intelligence had assured us were perfectly safe. In fact, for many World War II airmen, the term "military intelligence" still evokes laughter.

Later, in prison camp, with too much time on our hands, some unknown author wrote a tribute to military intelligence, which many of us who had been shot down read and appreciated:

Ode to S-2

S-2 is so amazing! They seem to have the knack,
Of knowing when, at what, is where—excepting fighters and flak!

S-2 is so ingenious! They seem to have the knack,
Of crediting all victories shot down by George–to Jack!

S-2 is so efficient! It seems it is their renown,
They get you quickly right to where you get yourself shot down!

S-2 is so unperturbed! They never flinch or frown,
They'll out fly any German ace, in any bar in town!

S-2 is so complex! They like to go on flings,
Before they leave for town each night, they borrow pilots' wings!

S-2 is so generous! They work for what they get,
To run the risk of map-osis or blonde or brunette!

S-2 is so valorous! They'd gladly take the air,
And fly all day for extra pay, in Flak Alley!

S-2 is so confident! They meet with great elation,
The enemy as he comes out, at the interrogation!

S-2 is so effective! They raise such commotion,
About our exploits in the air, that they get our promotions!

We would pile out of the briefing shack, get in jeeps and trucks, and ride to our planes. In the meantime, our mechanics had been up most of the night preflighting our aircraft. We would walk around our planes and talk with the crew chiefs about any concerns. We'd then strap ourselves in, start the engines, check the dials, and clamp our feet on the brakes to prevent any premature movement of the 10,000-pound plane. For these missions, we had 92 gallons of gas inside each wing, 100 gallons hanging under each wing, and another 85 gallons in a tank behind the pilot. We also had two 50-caliber guns in each wing with 300 rounds for each gun.

We had only one runway from which all four squadrons would take off. Two squadrons would take off from each end. After the magneto engine check, the planes would sit idling until takeoff time. The lead plane would taxi onto the runway, waiting for the tower to fire off a green flare exactly at takeoff time. The Group Leader would then start rolling down the runway. Number two would

follow close behind. Number three would move into place so he could follow. Fighting the turbulence of the preceding planes now became a challenge. This continued until sixteen planes and the two spares had taken off. It was then that the lead plane of the second squadron would start his takeoff from the other end of the same runway.

While awaiting takeoff, with that big eleven-foot prop spinning and those 1,500 horses pulling the plane, your pulse begins to race, especially when you look down the line and see the other fifteen planes in your squadron slowly easing forward to begin taxiing down the ramp. Canopies are open, and the noise is deafening but exhilarating. You just hope the bastard behind you doesn't let up on his brakes and chew your tail off, or that the so-and-so on your left has his gun switch off or his finger off the trigger so he doesn't blow you to smithereens. You sit at the end of the runway and wait, your plane throbbing and threatening to bolt. Your legs are tied in knots from clamping your feet on the brakes. Fumes and dust penetrate your oxygen mask. There you sit, locked in, unable to move, worrying about somebody's prop chewing on your left and your prop threatening the guy on your right. Finally, you look to your left and watch the 99th beginning to take off from the other end of the strip directly toward you. The first few guys pass over about fifty feet out in front of you. As number five and six begin to hit the turbulence of the previous guys, they wobble back and forth. You look up, and a P-51 sails over your head with about ten to fifteen feet to spare!

After the eighteen get off, sixteen plus two spares, it finally becomes our turn. Bubble Blue Leader wheels out and we turn and taxi out to take off behind him. Throttle forward, engine pulling sixty inches of mercury, mixture rich, using left main tank, mags checked, dials in the green, prop pitch low, throttle pushed forward, forced back in seat by the tremendous acceleration, watching airspeed, easing off a bit, watching the torque, queuing in on the element leader, cutting him off, while he's cutting off the flight leader who is cutting off the squadron leader, who is cutting off the group leader: a giant luftberry in the sky, made up of seventy-two circling planes. The group circles the field twice before everyone is ready to get into tight formation: Four squadrons, seventy-two planes, off to pick up B-17s or B-24s.

One of my most vivid memories of combat is sitting above those B-17s. It was always mind-boggling to look back as far as the eye could reach and see that ten

"Hitting the Blue."

to fifteen-mile string of bombers that might include as many as a thousand planes. Up above, you'd see the contrails of our P-51s zigzagging back and forth over the straight contrails of the bombers. Typically, if the B-17s were flying at 24,000 feet, the 99th Squadron would be at 25,000 feet, the 100th at 26,000 feet, the 101st at 27,000 feet, and the 302nd at 28,000 feet. Because the bombers were so much slower, each fighter squadron would zigzag back and forth at 220 mph over the B-17s, which were flying at 160 mph. Occasionally a squadron might be forced up to 32,000 feet, but in such thin air, one had to avoid sharp maneuvers, or the mushy controls might cause the plane to spin out.

So many things happen simultaneously: planes switching tanks, radios squawking, "Bogies (meaning unknown planes) at three o'clock," and then a loose, ragged formation automatically tightening when someone hollers, "Get the hell out of my ass!" Eyes get sharper, breathing becomes more rapid, heads weave right and left. Bubble Blue Leader comes in curt and sharp, "Bubble Blue, drop tanks on mark." Immediately you switch your fuel from wing tanks to internal. Most of us had already done so when we first heard someone holler, "Bogie." The sight of sixteen P-51s dropping tanks was spectacular: thirty-two silvery, bullet-shaped objects dropping like huge drops of rain, and often seeing the German planes turning away and refusing to come in.

Many escort missions were monotonous, five or six-hour rides, but they could also be exhilarating. I remember on my fourth or fifth mission our squadron got eight or nine kills. I didn't see a single one, because I was too busy flying my element's wing, protecting his rear end. Above all, there was a great feeling of relief when all our planes returned safely to base.

My most unforgettable mission was flying cover over the Ploesti oil fields. After we picked up our bombers at the border of Hungary and Romania, we encountered only sporadic anti-aircraft fire on the way to the target. Then, some fifteen or twenty miles ahead, I saw a huge black cloud, shaped like a hockey puck, from 20,000 feet to about 26,000 feet. I could see a series of fires and lots of smoke rising from the ground underneath it, which appeared to be an oil refinery complex. The B-17s flew out on a sixty-degree angle and then aimed directly for that black cloud. We pulled off to the left and orbited while they disappeared into the black cloud. Then, we saw four or five B-17s falling out of the bottom of the cloud, spinning down lazily, trailing smoke and flames. Unconsciously, I yelled, "Bail out, damn it! Get out of there!" Out of one of the planes I counted one, two, three chutes opening up. Then there was a big whoosh. The B-17 had exploded in a huge red ball of flames. Realism set in: three chutes had opened; that meant seven men had died, right there in front of my eyes. Seven men no longer existed. I threw up into my oxygen mask—at 31,000 feet. That experience—including my crew chief's refusing to clean my oxygen mask after I returned to base—burned itself into my mind.

I landed on the island of Vis twice, just off the coast of Yugoslavia. Vis was held by the Allies, and it saved a hell of a lot of planes that were low on fuel or shot up and could not make it back across the Adriatic to Italy. The airfield was

"Bringing Home a Cripple."

a literal boneyard. There were wrecked planes everywhere, mostly fighters and bombers that had barely made it back before crash landing. Both times I was forced to land on Vis my squadron had stayed with our bombers long past the allotted time. The fighter group that was supposed to rendezvous and relieve us had showed up late, which meant we didn't have enough fuel to make it home. I remember sitting on the wing of my plane in Vis surveying all the wrecked airplanes while the ground crew gassed me up. I also remember drinking a wretched cup of coffee, my first of the day, because we never drank coffee in the morning before a long mission that could last up to six hours. We did have a

small relief tube in the plane, but you couldn't get to your personal equipment through the parachute straps and your flying suit.

After every mission we were debriefed. Intelligence was always interested in determining whether what they had told us in the morning was helpful. Of course, what we actually experienced was almost always the opposite of what they had told us to expect.

I don't remember much else about camp life at Ramitelli, except that I still made my model airplanes. Even in wartime, my life settled into some kind of routine, at least until I was shot down and captured on August 12, 1944.

"'A' Flight All Present."

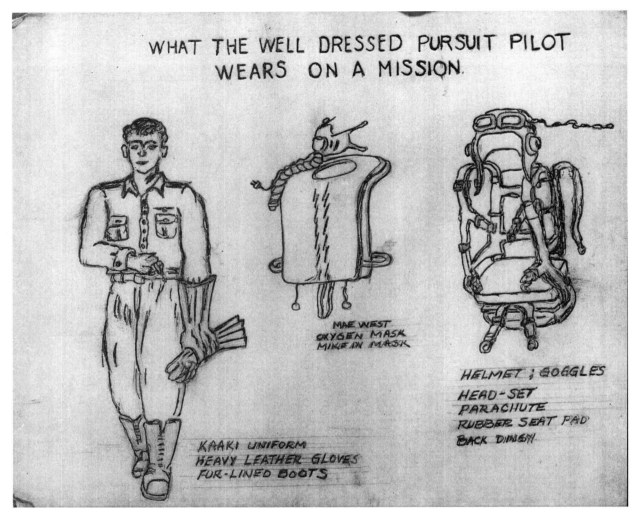

"*What the well-dressed*
pursuit pilot wears . . ."

5 Captured!

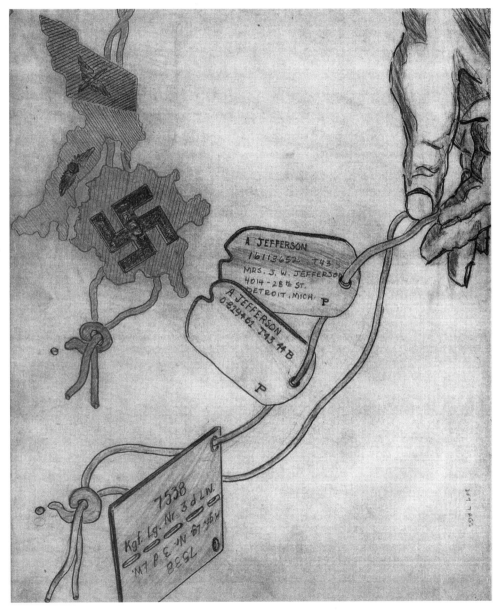

Hand and dog tags.

On August 12, 1944, I was a pilot with the 301st Fighter Squadron, 332nd Fighter Group, 15th Air Force. I was flying my nineteenth mission, which was to strafe and knock out radar stations at Toulon Harbor on the southern coast of France to prevent the Germans from detecting the Allied invasion ships, which three days later, as part of Operation Dragoon, would land between Marseilles and Nice.

It was a beautiful clear day, with unlimited visibility, when our sixteen P-51s flew in over the coast in four flights of four each. The first three sets of four went in, hit the target at low level, and flew out to sea. We were the last flight. As we dived in from 15,000 feet at about 400 knots, I was Tail-End Charlie, which meant I was the last plane to go in. When our squadron leader called for us to drop our hundred-gallon tanks, somehow my tanks got hung up and I was slow dropping them. In order to catch up, I had to push everything to the wall, with my airspeed almost redlined. I was pulling about sixty inches of manifold pressure, the plane was shaking and rocking, but I did get back into position just before our flight began to fire on the target.

Halfway down, I could see blinking red lights over the target; in fact, the entire side of the cliff in front of the radar towers was covered with anti-aircraft fire. About a thousand yards from the target, out of the corner of my eye, I saw Bob Daniels's number two plane take two direct hits. He began trailing black smoke and headed out to sea. I found out later he had elected to set down on the water, which was not advised, because the air scoop could pull the plane under water before the pilot could extricate himself. Nevertheless, Daniels got out and floated on the water until the Germans picked him up.

By this time, we were down to three hundred feet, flying at more than 400 mph. Looking ahead, I could see the first flight of four getting hits on the towers and veering out to sea. Right behind them came the second and third flights, which also got their hits and banked out to sea. Then we came into position. With the target in range, my ship was bucking and shaking. Anti-aircraft fire was coming up on all sides. My oil pressure and coolant temp needles were in the red, with everything else at the top of the green, about to go red.

As I passed over the target at about fifty feet, I felt a loud thump shake the plane. I glanced at the instrument panel, and now everything was in the red. I felt a tremendous rush of air. I looked up and there was a hole in the top of my canopy just in front of my head. I thought, "What the hell?" Fire and smoke were

Going in for the kill
at Toulon Harbor.

*Looking out my cockpit
and seeing Bob Daniels's
plane hit.*

filling the cockpit. I looked down and saw that flames were coming up through a hole in the floor between my feet and scorching my gloves and boots. I pulled up into a loop to get some altitude, jerked the red knob on the instrument panel, and popped the canopy. At the same time, I racked in the forward trim tab on the elevator with my left hand. At the top of the loop, I punched the safety belt release and let go of the stick. The forward trim tab was supposed to pitch the nose down, but because the plane was upside down, the nose went up abruptly and I was thrown out. I figure I got out at about eight hundred feet.

I can still see the tail, including the rivets, as it went whizzing by. I pulled the D-ring. I looked at it in my hand and thought, "Some SOB sold the silk." The rumor back at the base was that someone had been stealing the silk out of the parachutes and selling it to the Italians. So when my chute did not immediately open, I thought that had happened to me. But just then the chute popped, and all I could see was green. I fell through some trees and hit squarely on my feet and rolled over. I sustained cuts and bruises on my arms and legs. Fortunately, I was wearing paratrooper jump boots because they gave extra support to my ankles.

At the time, things are happening so fast you don't have time to get scared. It's only a couple of days later, when you have time to think about what happened, that it all hits you. Intelligence had told us French resistance fighters were in the area, so we were supposed to dig a hole, hide our parachute, and wait for the French to find us. Hell, I hit the ground, rolled over, and looked up into the muzzle of a Mauser and a German soldier saying, "Ja, Ja, Herr Leutnant. Für Sie ist der Krieg vorbei." ("Ah, yes, Lieutenant. For you the war is over.") I had landed right in the middle of the 20 mm gun crew that had shot me down.

The other guys in my flight had looked back and saw my plane go in, but they didn't see me get out. They thought I had bought the farm and reported me killed in action. My mother and dad subsequently received the dreaded KIA telegram. Not until several weeks later did the International Red Cross notify them that I was a prisoner of war.

The first things my captors took were my cigarettes, my Parker pen, and my wristwatch. They then transported me in a car several miles east of Toulon to a small villa overlooking the Mediterranean. A German officer was seated at a glass table on the veranda. I saluted because he had rank on his shoulders. In perfect English, he said, "Have a seat, lieutenant, and thanks for the Lucky

Parachuting from the wreckage of Margo.

A rough landing.

Strikes!" He spoke very formally and asked me how things were in the States. I replied, as S-2 had instructed us, with name, rank, and serial number. He ignored this and asked if I had ever been in Atlanta. I told him I hadn't, although, of course, I had spent four years attending Clark College. He talked about the black clubs on Auburn Avenue and the good times he had enjoyed in the various bars and hotels. He then asked if I had ever been in Washington, D.C. I again told him no, even though I had attended Howard University.

He then proceeded to tell me about his days at the University of Michigan, naming streets, fraternity houses, and restaurants. It turned out he had graduated from the University of Michigan in 1936, with a Ph.D. in political science. After returning to Germany, he was called into the army and eventually assigned to the anti-aircraft unit that shot me down. He was a jazz fan and talked about the Howard Theater and the Crystal Caverns nightclub in Washington, where all the black jazz artists appeared, and then he started talking about Detroit's Paradise Valley. His whole demeanor changed and he became much friendlier. He told me about boarding the Oakland streetcar next to the library behind the J. L. Hudson Department Store in downtown Detroit, and how it proceeded east on Adams, past the "Colored" YMCA and the Three Sixes Nightclub and then turned north on Hastings and then west on Forest Street, where Sonny Wilson's Bar was on the corner. He even named the bartenders and the girls across the street in the "hotel." For the next thirty minutes or so, I sat listening while he smoked my Lucky Strikes and excitedly told me about his Detroit experiences, especially about all the fun he had while drinking and carousing with the local girls. He finally said to me, "Some of the best times in my life were spent in the Valley. Let's hope this war ends soon so we can get back to the things that really matter." With that he offered me one of my cigarettes, shook my hand, then stood on the porch in a typical Nazi stance, watching silently and forlornly as they loaded me aboard a truck to be transported to a POW camp in Germany. I thought to myself, it really is a small world. At first, he had rubbed my feelings a little raw, hearing him speak about the "good" loving he received from our black girls back home. In the end, however, I was truly thankful for their efforts on behalf of the war. Truly thankful, indeed.

I have no idea what happened to him, but after I left I was taken to a Luftwaffe field about twenty miles north of Toulon and locked in a barracks room overnight. The next day, the Germans brought in Bob Daniels, whom they had picked up in the Mediterranean. Very early the next morning, which was August 14, the two of us, with two guards, departed for Marseilles by bus where we boarded a train and headed up the Rhone Valley to Orange. We rode on a flatbed car along with at least twenty 88 mm anti-aircraft guns, the artillery responsible for the terrific flak our bombers had to endure over Germany. Fortunately, no Allied planes spotted us. From Orange we got rides on wagons and trucks, and also did some walking before we reached Valence, where we stayed overnight in a barn that reeked of cows and sheep. While we were groping around the barn in the dark, we came across Richard Macon from the 302nd Squadron, who had been shot down on the same mission near Montpellier, about forty miles down the coast from Toulon. He was in bad shape and appeared to have a fractured neck because every time he moved abruptly, he passed out. We braced his neck and head to make them immovable. When we got him up the next morning, he had to walk very slowly, trying not to move his head.

The next day the three of us continued up the Rhone Valley toward Lyon in the back of a truck with our two guards. Naturally, we were a little concerned. We had heard that the Germans considered blacks to be apes and all kinds of other stereotypes. We knew what they thought about Jews. We had encountered some racism in Italy, although we later found out that was mostly due to white American soldiers telling the Italians terrible things about us. But our two regular army Wehrmacht guards saw us as officers, even celebrities, and treated us accordingly. They even shared their food with us, which consisted of grapes, melons, hard brown bread, margarine, and blood sausage they had bartered for with French civilians. Blood sausage is made from congealed animal blood, but I learned to relish it.

On August 20, we reached Oberursel, Germany, just outside of Frankfurt, but we only stayed there for a couple of days before we were moved some thirty miles north to Dulag Luft just northwest of Wetzler, which was the central interrogation center for captured airmen. Dulag Luft stands for Durchgangslager der Luftwaffe (air force transit camp). I was thoroughly searched, photographed, fingerprinted, and given POW number 7538. The photo depicts a tired, unshaven, dirty face that shows the results of what I had endured since my capture. In fact, I do look a bit like a *Luftgangster,* an "air gangster," as the Germans called Allied fliers.

During the four days I spent in Dulag Luft, I was kept in solitary confinement, though allowed my first shower, shave, sleep, and hot meal since being captured. This meal consisted of oatmeal, German bread, cocoa, and powdered eggs, some of which obviously came from a Red Cross parcel. It tasted good, especially since all I had eaten since my capture on the twelfth was the food our guards shared with us traveling up the Rhone.

During my third day in Dulag Luft, I was taken to an office to be interrogated. When I entered the room, I faced a German officer sitting behind a desk staring at me. In perfect English, but a bit too cordially, he said, "Have a seat, lieutenant." I sat down across the desk from him and noticed that he was thumbing

Alexander Jefferson's POW identification card.

through a large notebook, the cover of which stated, *332nd Fighter Group—Negroes—Red Tails*. Without saying a word, he slowly flipped through pages. I immediately recognized the photographs of several of the Tuskegee classes that had graduated before mine. Suddenly, he stopped and said, "Lieutenant, isn't this you?" He was pointing to my January 7, 1944, graduation class picture, taken at Tuskegee Army Air Field, and there I was, standing fifth from the right in the top row.

He proceeded to tell me my life story, and he seemed to know more about me than I knew about myself. He told me my father's social security number, his take-home pay, the taxes he paid on his home, all my grades at Clark College and Howard University, and even my sister's college grades. He told me about our mission over southern France, and, even more amazingly, he had my crew chief's ten-hour inspection on the plane I flew, which was completed the day before I was shot down. Some of this information was public record, but not the inspection or our mission. The Germans had to have had somebody at Ramitelli Air Base or higher up the line who was giving them information.

While he was telling me all this, I sat and smoked his cigarettes. Interestingly, he asked me no questions about tactics, targets, or equipment. He was very con-

6 Stalag Luft III

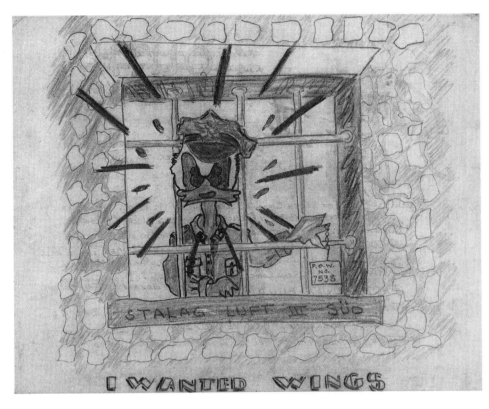

This drawing, which was originally done by another pilot, circulated around Stalag Luft III. Each of us made alterations. I added the service cap and the bars on the collar.

I tried to look on my captivity as just one among many extraordinary experiences. The only time I really became frightened was during the three-day train ride from Dulag Luft to Stalag Luft III. Daniels, Macon, and I were again escorted by two German guards with rifles. When the train stopped in a small town, and we walked through the station to catch another train, we were accosted by a group of Hitler Youth. They were singing some kind of marching song, but when they spotted us they began yelling obscenities and haranguing us. They called us *Luftgangster* (air gangsters) and *Terrorflieger* (pilots of terror) and all kinds of other things, which, fortunately, I did not understand. Scared? You're damn right I was scared. We had heard of downed Allied flying personnel being beaten and even murdered by angry German civilians. After all, what would American citizens have done to German airmen who had just bombed their homes and cities?

Our two guards were all but overwhelmed before they managed to get us through the station and onto the waiting train where they locked us in our compartment. These crazy youngsters were still running up and down the train platform, screaming and yelling at the top of their lungs. By this time some of the nearby civilians had also become aroused. We fully expected to be dragged off the train and killed. Our guards even had to threaten to shoot at the mob before the train finally pulled out of the station. It's funny, but I was never really frightened when I was shot down or during my eight and a half months in captivity, but in that damn train station I was scared to death!

When we arrived at Stalag Luft III on August 26, 1944, Richard Macon was immediately sent to the camp hospital, and Robert Daniels was assigned to a room in another barracks. After they left, I had quite a surprise. The camp was already overcrowded, so each barracks room had to choose a new roommate.

Approximately two hundred of us new POWs were lined up, and a representative from each room walked down the line and picked out a new roommate. A dyed-in-the-wool cracker with the deepest southern drawl imaginable walked up to me and said, "Ah think I'll take this boy." I was naturally very apprehensive, thinking that I had not come all the way from the USA to be with a bunch of rednecks. I really wanted to reject what I was sure would simply result in discrimination and humiliation. However, standing immediately behind this good ole boy was an American full bird colonel. He motioned and said, "Lieutenant, you go with him." I saluted and went off to my assigned room. What I found was a real hodgepodge of ethnicities: there were two or three southerners, a

Jew, a couple of guys from Brooklyn, a couple more from God knows where, and Hal Erickson who was from Detroit. I was the only black.

I soon discovered why they had chosen me. Their room happened to house escape materials, and they wanted to make sure they didn't get a German plant or an American turncoat. They later told me, "We knew we could trust you." I thought it then and have said it many times since, "Ain't that a bitch!" At home, black soldiers caught hell from SOBs just like the guy who had selected me. Now, five thousand miles from home, they can trust a black man because they are scared to death of a strange white face. Ain't that a bitch!

Stalag Luft III was a huge prison camp located near Sagan, a town of some 25,000 inhabitants, located about ninety miles southeast of Berlin on the Bóbr River, which itself was a tributary of the Oder. Today the town belongs to Poland. When Luft III opened in April 1942, it housed primarily British airmen and Commonwealth prisoners, but by the time I arrived on August 26, 1944, the majority of Stalag Luft III prisoners were American airmen.

The comparatively principled Luftwaffe administered Stalag Luft III. I know of no brutal treatment of American or English officers, with the exception of the SS's execution of the fifty English officers who were captured after they escaped through a tunnel in "The Great Escape," as it was called in at least two books and one very successful Hollywood film.

When I arrived, the camp consisted of only the North, South, and West compounds. When we eventually evacuated the camp on January 29, 1945, it had grown to a sprawling complex of six compounds and more than ten thousand prisoners. The entire camp was surrounded by two barbed-wire fences. The space between these two fences was considered no-man's land, and any prisoner could be shot if he entered this space. Thirty feet inside the ten-foot fence was a guard rail. This was the perimeter that prisoners would walk—"pounding the perimeter"—thrashing out beefs, gripes, philosophy, and likes and dislikes. This is where Frank Haddick and I formed a lasting friendship. We walked many a mile around that $^{6}/_{10}$-mile boundary.

I was housed in Room 8, Block 128, which was our barracks building in South Compound. The room itself was 16 × 16 feet, with two triple bunks and two double bunks. And, in spite of my initial reservations, my roommates turned out to be extremely open-minded. Of course, with our varied backgrounds we did have lots of interesting discussions concerning race and discrimination, but we

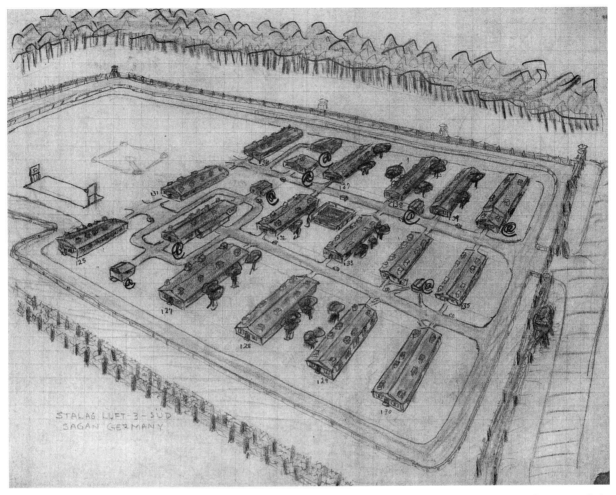

Layout of compounds in Stalag Luft III.

SOUTH

Stalag Luft III

Sagan. Germany
AS OF DEC 25, 1944

Rechts: VIEW OF SOUTH CMPD. AS SEEN BY FW-190 PILOTS WHO OFTEN BUZZ US. SURROUNDED BY 2 FENCES (BARBED WIRE OF COURSE).

@ ABORTS; TRURLY OUTDOOR TYPE ACCOMIDATING 30 MEN.

@ COOK HOUSE; ADMIN. OFFICES IN NO. END; COL. MESS IN SO. END. CENTER HOUSES LARGE BOILERS FOR SOUP AND HOT WATER.

@ WASH HOUSE; ROW CONCRETE SLAB + COLD H₂O + GI SOAP + BRUSH + ARM GREASE = CLEAN CLOTHS.

@ HOT SHOWER BUILDING!.

TRACK AROUND CAMP IS KNOWN AS THE PERIMETER. BEYOND THE RAIL AROUND IT "TIS VERBOTEN"!

@ THEATER; GEN ROOM + CLASS ROOMS ARE IN NORTH END.

South Compound, Stalag Luft III

Der Abort (latrine, meant to accommodate thirty men)

Cook House (administrative offices in north end; large boilers in center for heating soup and hot water)

Wash House (cold water)

Hot Shower Building

Theater (also contained classrooms and library)

Block 128, Jefferson's "home"

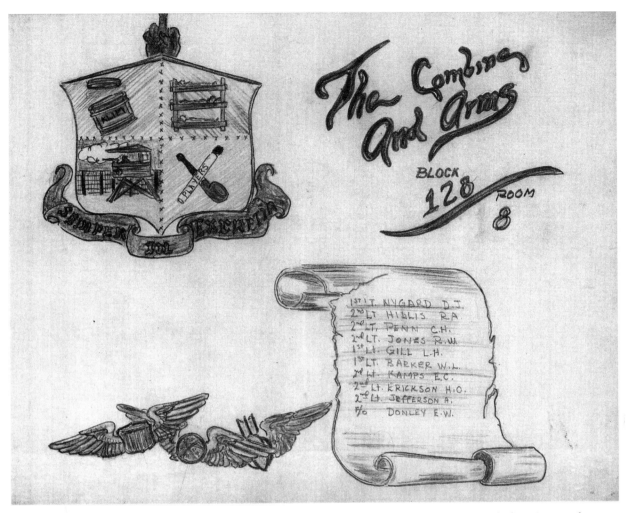

Block 128's coat of arms.

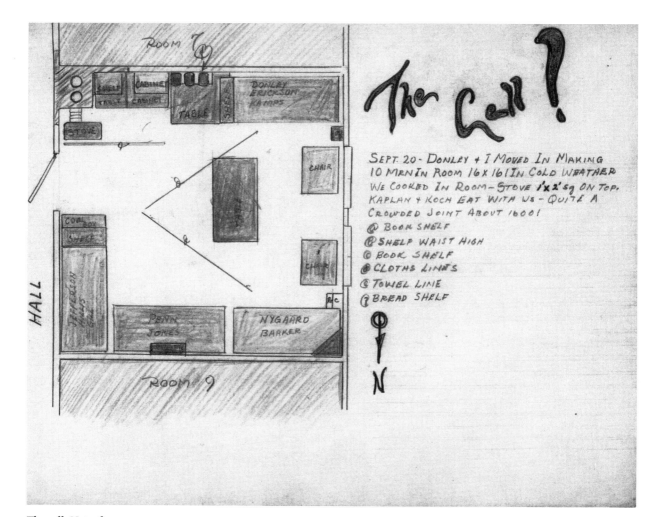

The cell. Note the names on the bunks—Harold E. Erickson and Louis Gill. Both are now residents of Livonia, Michigan, a suburb of Detroit. Gill and I attend the weekly POW sessions at the Veterans' Hospital.

Room 8, Block 128.

Jefferson sketches his bunkmates from his top-bunk vantage.

Wash Day.

The boys of
Block 128 knitting.

all came to respect one another. I even drew a coat of arms for our guys. Of course, we tried not to take things too seriously, as you can tell by the "Fickle Finger of Fate" located at the top of our shield and our motto, "Semper in Excretia." You can also tell by some of my room drawings that we weren't the best of housekeepers.

We had a nearby washhouse, where we did most of our washing in cold water in tin basins. We occasionally got to take a shower in a different building. We had soap in our Red Cross parcels so we were able to keep ourselves relatively clean, which was very important because body lice were everywhere, as well as various other creepy and crawling vermin. Of course, military discipline also helped inspire us to keep ourselves clean.

I drew lots of pictures to keep from being bored. The International Red Cross supplied us with paper, pencils, pens, and ink. They also sent us all kinds of games, as well as a wide variety of sporting equipment so we could play baseball, basketball, and even soccer. I played lots of cards and I spent a lot of time read-

The washroom.

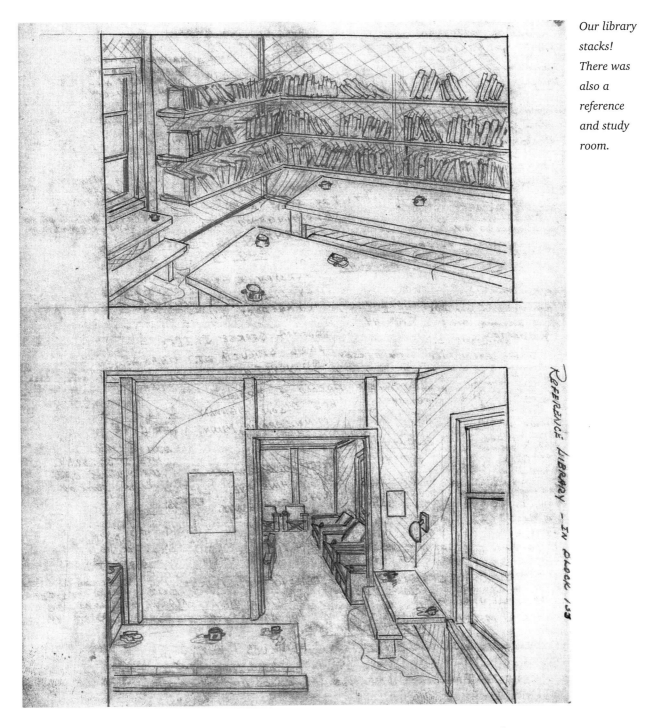

Our library stacks! There was also a reference and study room.

REFERENCE LIBRARY — IN BLOCK 155

ing. We had a fabulous library in Stalag Luft III containing several thousand volumes. Some of the men had been there for several years and their families had sent them books. The Red Cross also supplied books. I must have read fifty or sixty different books during my five months in Stalag Luft III.

There were twelve of us Tuskegee Airmen in Luft III. I was in the South Compound with Woody Morgan, Robert Daniels, and Richard Macon, after he got out of the hospital. Scotty Halfcock and Lewis Smith were in the West Compound. The other six were in either Center or North Camp. The North Compound held primarily British prisoners.

Surprisingly, there were few fighter pilots in Stalag Luft III. Most American prisoners had flown bombers. Of course, as Tuskegee Airmen, we were held in high esteem. We were also a bit older and more mature. All of us were college graduates, although some of the white pilots were not.

Did I experience any overt racism or general resentment on the part of the white POWs? Understandably, I felt an undercurrent of hesitancy and a kind of guarded inquisitiveness. Some of these men had been prisoners for more than two years and had no idea that blacks were now pilots and officers in the Army Air Corps. This was very strange to them, but then one day a B-17 crewmember arrived in Stalag Luft III. When he spotted me, he ran over, grabbed and hugged me, and exclaimed, "You're a Red Tail! You goddamn Red Tails are the best damned unit! If the Red Tails had been with us, we'd have made it back home! You guys saved our asses so many times!" After that encounter, the reputation of the 332nd Fighter Group spread quickly throughout the camp.

The camp was very well organized. After all, we were still in the military. The senior officer for the Americans was Colonel Charles G. Goodrich, and he enforced military discipline straight down the line. Each morning and evening all POWs had to fall out for *Appell* (roll call). Colonel Goodrich would form us into blocks on the parade ground. *Appell* usually took about thirty minutes, unless the count was off, which meant each of us would be scrutinized to make sure we matched the photo on our German ID card. This could take two or three hours, which was not all that pleasant in freezing weather.

The Geneva Convention mandated that officers were not to work. Nevertheless, we would occasionally volunteer to do something that would help make life easier for us. For example, the land on which Stalag Luft III was constructed had previously been a pine forest, and there were still lots of stumps, especially near

Camp stump puller.

the athletic field where we were allowed to play baseball and various other games. We wanted them out, so we constructed a Rube Goldberg contraption that allowed us to get enough leverage to pull out the stumps. I was far too small to be of much help, but I did sketch the whole affair.

In the beginning we all dreamed of wine, women, song, and food. After the first week, we forgot about the wine; next we forgot about the song; after four or five more weeks, we forgot about the women; but we never forget about food.

Each barracks had a stove to serve 120 men. Each room was assigned a time each day to use the stove for baking or the general preparation of meals. We also had a small stove in our room we could use when some kind of fuel was available.

We augmented our German rations with our Red Cross parcels, which arrived more or less on a regular basis, although not after we were moved to Stalag VIIA in Moosburg. These were lifesavers, but the guys still dreamed of some good old home cooking.

As the war wound down and transportation became a severe problem, we received fewer and fewer Red Cross parcels. Instead of each man receiving his own parcel each week, he now had to share it with others, if indeed the parcels got through at all. The contents of the parcels differed, depending on the country of origin, but typically they contained a wide variety of items.

Necessity is the mother of invention, and many of the inventions the guys came up with were truly remarkable. For example, using the metal from a KLIM can, which contained powdered milk, they produced all kinds of imaginative things. We called this process "tingenuity."

We often dreamed of escape, but we knew this was not a realistic possibility, although some men certainly tried. After all, most of us did not speak German, and certainly no one would have mistaken me for a German. We also knew about the Great Escape and the execution of the fifty prisoners who were caught. Yes, executing a prisoner for attempting an escape was a violation of the Geneva Convention, but that certainly did not help those killed by the SS. In my drawing, two prisoners have been caught red-handed by a "ferret," which is what we called the guards who sneaked around looking for trouble. Notice the wire cutters and the piece of the fence the boys had snipped. They spent a week in the cooler on bread and water for their transgressions.

Sometimes, when we were out for morning *Appell* or just wandering around,

Kriegie brew.

Dreaming of women.

The barracks stove.

Two men and their Red Cross parcels.

A lone Red Cross parcel.

TINGENUITY +

ADD TO THE INGENUITY OF THE KRIEGEFANGENEN, A PILE OF EMPTY KLIM TINS AND THE ARTISTRY OF THE "TIN BASHER" — THE RESULT WILL SATISFY MANY NEEDS OF THE P.O.W.

OUR OWN DANNY HAS PROVIDED ROOM 8 WITH PANS — AN OVEN — SPUD PEELER — CLOTHS PRANGER — COFFEE POT — CARROT SLICER ETC.

A FEW EXAMPLES OF SOUTH CMPD. PRODUCTS; A CLOCK FACE, GERMAN DOLLAR WATCH WORKS WITHIN; AN ACCURATE ZINC-TIN THERMOMETER, WITH CENTIGRADE AND FARENHEIT SCALES; A BAROMETER; CRACKER-GRINDER; SAND FILLED FLAT-IRONS; TIN SUIT-CASES; BLOW TORCHES FOR SOLDERING (SOLDER EXTRACTED BIT BY BIT FROM TOP OF ROAST-BEEF CANS; TEA STRAINERS; PICTURE FRAMES; ET CETERA. PLUS KRIEGIE BURNERS — LITTLE GIANTS — BURN CARDBOAD — BEDBOARDS — PAPER — OPERATE ON GAS PRINCIPAL BLOWERS ATTACHED — WHITE HOT HEAT

Tingenious inventions.

A ferret on the hunt.

A buzz job from the
Luftwaffe.

a German FW-190 would buzz the camp, I suppose to impress us pilots with his flying skills.

For someone in captivity, Saturday nights were always tough. There you sat, slumped over, wondering what the guys were doing back home and if they were getting all the girls.

Sleeping was always a popular pastime for POWs, especially on Sunday morning, when we were sometimes allowed extra time in the sack.

Sleep, however, was often a mixed blessing. It was wonderful when you dreamed of all the good times you were planning to enjoy when you got back home, but more often sleep resulted in nightmares about the horrors of combat, including casualties, captivity, and death.

Of course, there were also daytime nightmares when we wondered if our sweethearts were remaining faithful. All kinds of fearsome images clouded our minds, especially about the lurid and eager creatures on the home front who might be courting our girlfriends.

I have no idea who was the original author of "The Draft Dodger." I just kept a copy of it when it passed through our barracks.

Mail was all-important. I started writing letters home as soon as I was captured. My family eventually got all of them, but, unfortunately, I never got any of their letters. Until the end of October 1944, they feared I had been killed in action. Then there was some kind of mix-up in the mail, so my mail never did catch up with me.

For those who did receive letters, there was nothing crueler than receiving the proverbial "Dear John letter." For such unfortunate prisoners, their world had come to a double end.

We had access to a German-language newspaper called *Der Beobachter* (*The Observer*). Of course, most of us couldn't read the articles, unless someone translated them for us. The cartoons were much easier to understand, and I traced several of them by holding them up to the window.

The craziest thing about my five months in Stalag Luft III was that I was never really scared. Maybe I was too dumb to be scared, but somehow I psychologically understood that I was just going to have to sit out my captivity.

Like most of the POW camps, we had radios in Stalag Luft III. The guys either constructed them, as they did everything else, from materials taken from Red Cross parcels, or the radios had been smuggled into camp. These radios allowed

Saturday night blues.

Sleep.

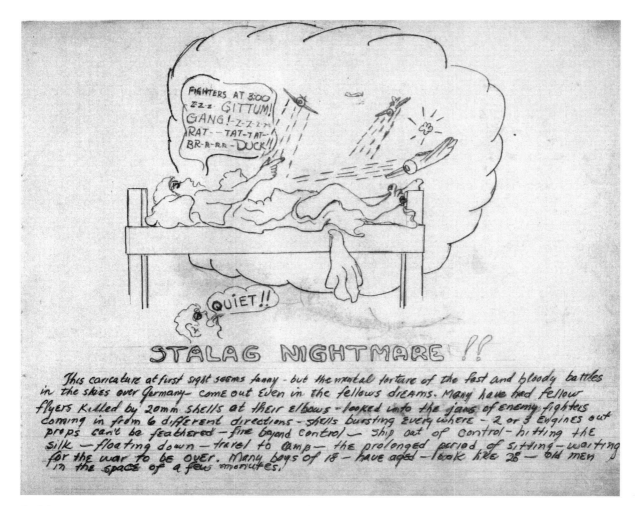

A nightmare.

Daytime nightmares.

Daytime nightmares.

The Draft
Dodger

I'M WRITING THIS SHORT LETTER,
AND EVERY WORD IS TRUE.
    DON'T LOOK AWAY, DRAFT DODGER,
FOR IT'S ADDRESSED TO YOU,
    YOU FEEL AT EASE, IN NO DANGER,
BACK IN THE OLD HOME TOWN.
    YOU COOKED UP SOME PITIFUL STORY
SO YOUR DRAFT BOARD WOULD TURN YOU DOWN
    YOU NEVER THINK OF REAL MEN,
WHO LEAVE HOME EVERY DAY,
    YOU THINK ONLY OF THEIR GIRL FRIENDS
THAT YOU TAKE INWHILE THEY'RE AWAY,
    YOU SIT HOME AND READ YOUR PAPER
YOU JUMP AND YELL — "WE'LL WIN,"
    JUST WHERE DO YOU GET THAT "WE" STUFF?
THE WAR WILL BE WON BY MEN.
    JUST WHAT DO YOU THINK DRAFT DODGER?
THAT THIS FREE-NATION WOULD DO?,
    IF ALL THE MEN WERE SLACKERS,
AND SCARED TO FIGHT, LIKE YOU?
    WELL, I GUESS THAT'S ALL, MR, SLACKER,
I SUPPOSE YOUR FACE IS RED.
    AMERICA IS NO PLACE FOR YOUR KIND,
AND I MEAN EVERY WORD I SAID.

"Dear Lieutenant . . ."

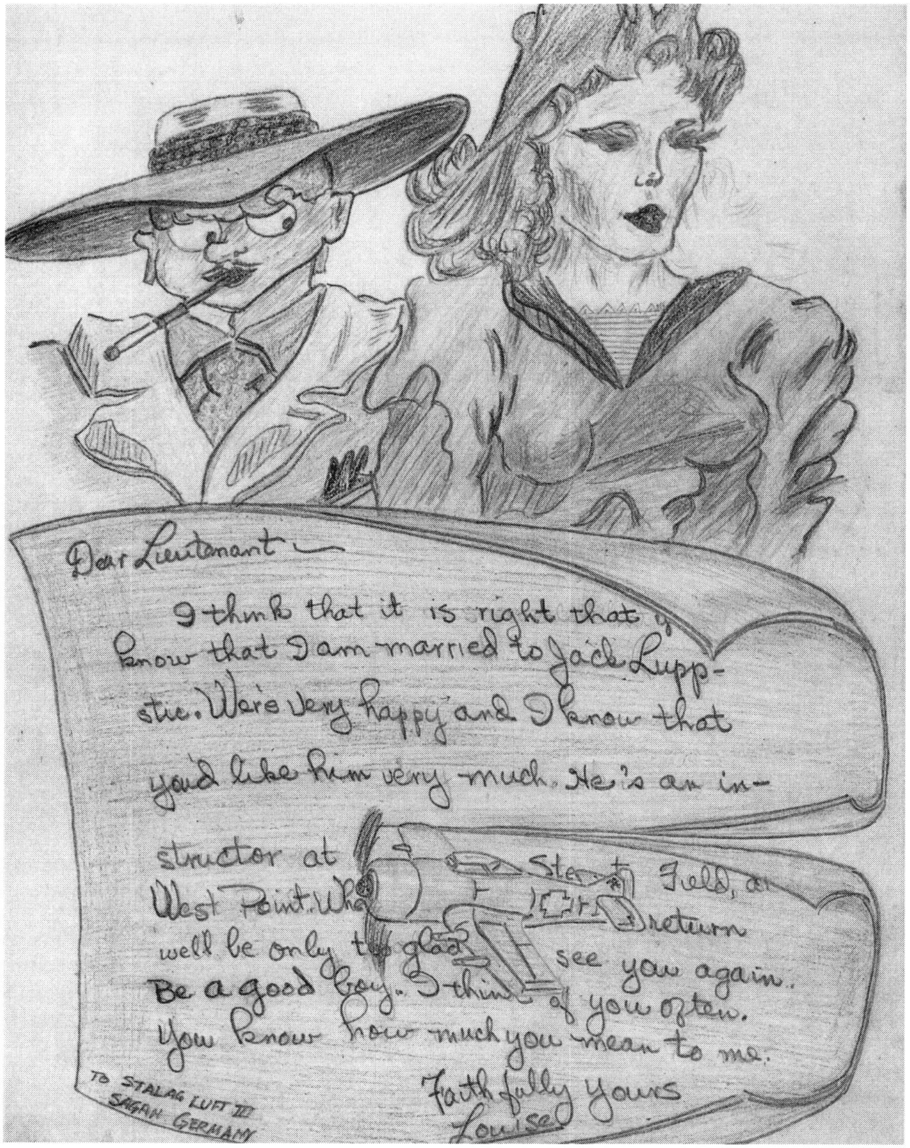

German cartoon: "Roosevelt prays: 'Dear God, bless our profits that our brave boys have not died in vain.'" Notice Roosevelt's Semitic advisers.

German cartoon: "USA: air gangsters murder European children." "Oh the humanity" is written on the blackboard; the lower caption reads, "The final lesson."

German cartoon: "Roosevelt's low-altitude war against women and children." Notice "Murder, Inc." written on the side of the American plane and Roosevelt's embracing of the Bible and the black pilot.

German cartoon: "After the final descent of the air gangsters: 'Damn, something must have gone wrong to keep us from our appointed rounds.'"

The cookhouse wall.

us to keep up with the war news. The Germans also maintained a bulletin board on the cookhouse wall, which contained all kinds of informational items, such as forthcoming athletic contests and dramatic and musical presentations. There was also a loudspeaker on the wall for various announcements. Finally, there was a map that showed the progress of the war. Of course, its depiction of the front lines was always two or three days old, so our radios were more current.

With all the information we had at our disposal, we were very much aware that the Russians were pushing back the German army and that the war would soon be over, but we didn't know exactly when. We also realized that it would likely be the Russian army that liberated us, but, because the Germans also knew this, on the very cold night of January 27, 1945, the camp officials forced us to evacuate Stalag Luft III.

7 Stalag VIIA and Liberation

When the Russian army started its final winter offensive through Poland and into Germany during the latter part of January 1945, temperatures were at record lows, with lots of snow on the ground. We knew from our radios and the cookhouse map that the Russians had taken Warsaw and Krakow and were advancing toward us. Then, on the evening of January 27, 1945, while we were watching the play *You Can't Take It With You*, put on by our fellow prisoners in the camp theater, Colonel Goodrich came in and announced that we had thirty minutes to pack up and be ready to evacuate the camp.

The Luftwaffe officers in charge of our camp simply could not allow several thousand highly trained Allied airmen to be rescued by the advancing Russians, so we were ordered to fall out for a forced march. We were told to carry nothing with us except food and clothing. Word was passed down to take sustaining types of food such as sugar, candy bars, and raisins rather than such items as powdered milk or potatoes. We rushed about getting our packs together in a kind of controlled pandemonium. We then put on as many items of clothing as we thought we could wear and still walk.

We did not know precisely where we were going, but we knew we were headed southwest toward the British and American lines and that the Russians were fast closing on us from the east. Spirits were high, but many of the men gorged themselves on food they had hoarded away and now could not take with them. Not surprisingly, they became sick, because their shrunken stomachs could not handle such large amounts of food, and this weakened them for the march.

Temperatures had dropped to 10 to 15 degrees below zero, and there were six to eight inches of newly fallen snow on the ground the night we left. Many of the men pulled their belongings on hastily improvised sleds, but when some of their buddies began to fall out, exhausted from the pace and their weakened physical condition, they allowed them to ride on their makeshift sleds, although they themselves were not in much better shape. Soon, exhausted men began throwing away letters, photographs, books, and all kinds of other personal items to lighten their loads.

I can still feel the bitter cold when my buddies from Room 8 and I started out walking at 11:00 that night. As far as the eye could see, there was a slow-moving column of men disappearing in the distance, and there were thousands more who would follow us out the gate later that night and the next morning. Our guards belonged to the Volksturm, or People's Guard, made up of old men in their sixties and seventies who suffered much more than we did. In fact, it was not unusual for a *Kriegie* to help carry the rifle of one of these old guards who was having great difficulty keeping up. I saw several guards fall out from exhaustion, but no one seemed to pay much attention to them, and they probably froze to death. Fortunately for us, the Red Cross had recently provided us with new shoes, heavy socks, gloves, scarves, and overcoats.

We didn't dare stop to rest because we had to keep moving to keep warm. We walked all that first night, covering some thirty kilometers to Grosse Stalle, arriving at 10:00 the next morning. We rested in barns until late that afternoon. Although I was dead tired, I jotted down in my small notebook the names of the small towns we passed through and the mileage that showed up periodically on the road signs.

We started walking again that second evening, and this was the most excruciating part of the entire journey. The temperature was still bone-chilling, at least ten degrees below zero, with a wind chill that made it feel even colder. Many of the guys will remember the long flat stretch of land where the cold wind hit us head on and seemed to go right through us. The only food we had was what we carried with us. Then the land became very hilly, and things really got rough. Clearly, we were too exhausted, hungry, and physically weakened to endure the demands of a forced march.

We arrived in Muskau at two in the morning of the 29th, after now having covered approximately fifty-five kilometers. We stayed in a large brick factory where we were able at least to dry our socks, fix our shoes and gloves, and get a little rest. It was warm and dry, and we were even able to wash. We also got our first German issue of black bread and margarine. Our rest was all too brief because the prisoners who had left Stalag Luft III after we did were pushing their way behind us.

After a rest of about eight hours, we left for the tiny village of Graustein, about twenty-five kilometers away, at 8:30 in the morning and arrived at 6:00 in the evening. We were assigned to a barn where we slept, crowded on top of each other for warmth. We left the next morning at 8:30 and arrived three hours later in Spremberg, which was a large town a few miles to the south. We were briefly housed in a brick building that someone said had been a Gestapo training school, before we left at 8:00 that evening by train for Moosburg and Stalag VIIA. In our exhausted condition, we were loaded on filthy and terribly crowded cattle cars for a two-day "ride" to Moosburg, which was located just northeast of Munich. These were the infamous "40 & 8" boxcars, which were supposed to have enough room for forty men or eight horses, but we were packed in some eighty men to a car. The trip across Germany was excruciating. We were so crowded that some of us had to stand while others rested. We had no food, water, heat, or room to stretch our legs. When we did get a chance to sit down, we had to sit in the animal excrement of the previous occupants. Some boxcars had "indoor plumbing," which consisted of a small tin can that quickly over-flowed. Some cars had no such can, so the armed guards permitted us to drop our pants and relieve ourselves when we stopped, generally at train stations in towns such as Chemnitz, Mosel, and Regensburg, and usually in full view of women and children. There we were, rows of POW "mooners"!

We arrived at Stalag VIIA at Moosburg on February 3, 1945. The place was a nightmare, with tens of thousands of men arriving from other prison camps. There was insufficient housing and very poor sanitary conditions. We were de-loused, and initially assigned to large tents for two days that held 250 men each. We slept on the ground, which was covered with wood shavings, in our clothing, under blankets they gave us. We were then put in 180-foot barracks that held 225 men. The barracks were dingy, stucco-walled, and poorly lighted. We had the usual three-tiered, side-by-side, wooden-framed bunks, with a cotton sack filled with straw for a mattress. Everything was filthy and so infested with bed-bugs, fleas, and other vermin that we decided to go back outside and sleep in the tents.

I drew only one sketch of the barracks in Stalag VIIA. As I look at this drawing today, I must say that it in no way captures the dreadful conditions we were forced to endure.

The Germans provided us with no cooking facilities, and the little food they gave us consisted of watery soup and black bread with slices of cheese, marga-rine, or blood sausage, but we did receive our first Red Cross food parcels since leaving Sagan. However, over the next few months, these parcels arrived infrequently, and when they did, each man often received only a part of a parcel. We cooked our food on burners and blowers we made out of tin cans, Red Cross boxes, and wire. A small piece of wood the size of your hand provided enough heat to boil water for five men for tea or soup, and for fuel we burned the bed boards, inner flooring of the barracks, and anything else we could scavenge.

We had pit toilets that quickly filled up and overflowed, sending their effluents out onto the ground and into our living areas. To make matters worse, the majority of us were suffering from diarrhea.

Stalag VIIA held approximately 100,000 Allied POWs, including some 45,000 Americans. Our immediate neighbors were turbaned Indians. Across the fence from us were Poles and Russians and other prisoners whom the Germans treated worse than cattle. However, we all suffered hunger pangs, a lack of heat, and even minimal medical care. The lice and fleas also did not discriminate.

One day we heard the unmistakable roar of P-51s flying at treetop levels. Someone came running by and yelled, "Hey, Jeff, there are a bunch of Red-Tailed P-51s in a square traffic pattern, taking turns shooting at something on the ground!" The entire camp ran out in the compound, yelling and jumping up and down, shouting and clapping our hands. The P-51s were in a luftberry, shooting up the Moosburg Train Station. These Red-Tails were from the 332nd Fighter Group—my unit!

Our days were pretty much taken up with watching our planes fly overhead and waiting for our Red Cross parcels to arrive. We could hear the loud explosions when our heavies hit Munich, which was less than twenty miles southwest of us. This always made us feel good, but our emotions ran in the opposite direction when we witnessed one of our planes go down. We were also on an emotional roller coaster with our Red Cross food packages. I remember in late February being depressed because we supposedly had only enough food parcels to last a week. But then our spirits soared over a rumor that full parcels from Switzerland would soon be arriving, which might mean we would have one man to a parcel instead of two, three, or even four.

Rumors kept us going, especially as the front lines closed in on us. Each day we heard reports on how close our troops were to Moosburg. Of course, we wondered if the Germans would move us again, but on April 24 we were told we would not be moved, although Patton and his troops were supposedly only forty kilometers away. Four days later we knew we weren't going anywhere because

the guards started to pack their belongings. The next morning there was no *Appell*. A guard told us about a Munich uprising and a huge tank battle only ten kilometers away. By that time, we could also hear the guns and see flares.

April 29, 1945! Liberation! At 9:00 in the morning the BBC reported Germany's unconditional surrender. At 10:00 a P-51 buzzed the camp at a hundred feet. P-47s dive-bombed Moosburg only a mile away. We could hear gunfire just down the street from our main gate, and some of our guys were hit. At 11:45, several large American tanks and some line soldiers arrived at our main gate. German soldiers were at the other end of the camp, and a small skirmish erupted. A camp officer named Gladovich, who always treated us well and who after the war even attended some American POW reunions, ran out waving a white flag. At 12:42, the American flag was raised over the town of Moosburg. A few minutes later we raised the American flag over the main gate of Stalag VIIA! One of the first things I did, once I knew the Germans were gone, was go to the camp headquar-

Red-Tails shooting up the Moosburg train station

Rumors.

ters building and take my German ID card out of the file (see page 60). A lot of other guys did the same thing.

At precisely 1400 hours, or 2:00 in the afternoon, a Sherman tank from George Patton's 14th Armored Division and an army jeep pulled into the camp. On May 1, General Patton himself arrived, followed by several generals and colonels. The yelling and applause were thunderous. Some of us accompanied Patton on a tour of the camp. He entered one of the filthy barracks and asked if it was for NCOs. When we told him, no, that these were officers' quarters, he nearly had a hemorrhage. No mattresses, and three blankets and one water pump for three hundred men! He ordered food to be immediately brought in from Moosburg. A U.S. Army food kitchen arrived the next day and provided hot food for us by 4:00 in the afternoon. Cognac, wine, and champagne also mysteriously appeared. It was announced that in seven to nine days we would be on our way to England and that shortly after that we would be heading home. A payroll truck also rolled into camp, and all we had to do was sign our name and receive $80.00.

According to my notebook, on May 3 I hitched a ride in a jeep and followed the American forces south to Dachau. I had heard there were a lot of dead bodies down the road, and I wanted to find out what that was all about. As we got closer to Dachau, I detected a nauseating odor, in the same way you can smell a barbecue on a warm summer day. Of course, this was the sickening smell of burned human flesh. The ovens were still warm when we entered Dachau.

The Dachau barracks were indescribable. There were thousands of striped-clothed skeletons lying on bunks or just milling around, and their sunken, hollow, vacant eyes still haunt me. Elsewhere, we found tables piled high with human hair and dental fixtures. There were corpses everywhere. Not surprisingly, I got violently ill.

A bulldozer gouged out a trench approximately two hundred feet long by twenty feet wide. The former German guards were then forced to throw in the dead bodies, many of which were in various states of decay. Next, they spread lime over the corpses and covered them with dirt. I can tell you, whatever has been said or printed about Dachau, no one can fully or adequately describe what we found there.

We left Moosburg by truck at 8:00 in the morning of May 9 and drove to Landshut, about fifty kilometers to the northeast. From there we flew to Verdun

Liberation Day in Stalag VIIA, April 29, 1945. Alexander Jefferson is standing in the lower left corner, facing the camera. U.S. Army photo.

on C-47s. After a two-week visit to Paris, about which I remember little except that the French women in Pigalle treated us like kings, we ended up on May 19 at Camp Lucky Strike, not far from the harbor at Le Havre. We were deloused, showered, given a typhus shot and a mock 64 (physical exam), processed, and assigned to tents in Area 23 where we got plenty of fine chow, including hard-boiled eggs, jam, and coffee.

On May 21 we went by truck to Le Havre and boarded the *USS Lejeune,* which was a navy transport. As a second lieutenant, I got the usual shaft and had to bunk down in the hole. We landed at Southampton, England, on May 23 and took on board some nurses and hospital cases. The next day we left for the States in a convoy of four troop ships, five destroyers, one flat top, and ten to fifteen Liberty ships.

We steamed into New York on June 7. The ship's horns were blasting and all of us were shouting at the top of our lungs. Spirits soared when the skyline of New York came into focus, and rose even higher when we spotted the Statue of

Liberty and finally docked. What a feeling of indescribable jubilation! But then, going down the gangplank, a short, smug, white buck private shouted, "Whites to the right, niggers to the left."

It was very discouraging, upon returning to the United States, to find racism, segregation, and other social ills alive and well. I knew then I was back home.

8 Civilian!

Tuskegee instrument instructors, 1945.

After a stay of two days at Fort Dix, New Jersey, and a leave of ten days followed by processing and reassignment in Atlantic City, I was assigned on August 25, 1945, to the Tuskegee Army Air Field as an instrument instructor in advanced training. A few months later, I was given additional duties as a flying instructor. I was making the princely sum of $250 a month, and life at postwar Tuskegee was absolute heaven. I loved flying during the day and partying most of the rest of the time.

Then one day I noticed a gorgeous bit of Alabama pulchritude flitting up and down the flight line. Her name was Adella McDonald, and she was a parachute rigger. When I first saw her, she was servicing parachutes for the various facilities at the airfield. Her co-worker was Winifred Davis, whose son, Major General Russell Davis, recently retired as commander of the Air National Guard. Well, one thing led to another, and Adella and I were married on October 16, 1946.

By this time, the military had closed the Tuskegee Army Air Base, and the 332nd and I had been transferred to Lockbourne Army Air Base in Columbus, Ohio. By 1947, the military had stepped up the reduction of its forces, and many of us were riffed from active duty. I was discharged on January 16, 1947, but I did go into the Air Force Reserve, from which I retired in 1969 with the rank of lieutenant colonel. During my last three years in the Reserves, I was Staff Operations and Training Officer of the 90th Air Force Recovery Squadron at Willow Run Airport, just west of Detroit.

When Adella and I moved to Detroit in 1947 to begin our lives as civilians, my immediate prospects were not very promising. I desperately needed a job to support my new wife, but every time I applied for a position, I was told I was "overqualified." I was even turned down for a job washing test tubes at pharmaceutical giant Parke Davis. I had no better luck at Semmet Solvay, which was a fuel processing facility. While waiting to be interviewed at Semmet Solvay, I struck up a conversation with a young white boy who sat down next to me. I learned that he had just finished Chadsey High School, from where I had graduated nineteen years earlier. When I was called in for my interview, I suggested we meet afterward and go out for a cup of coffee. Once again I was told I was "overqualified" for the position. When the young man came out from his interview, he told

Adella McDonald-Tucker Jefferson.

me he had been offered the job that consisted of running the same kind of carbon analysis test on steel that I had performed five years earlier, after graduating from Clark.

I then decided to go back to school, believing that if I became even more qualified, a place in industry would surely open up. I made an appointment with Wayne State University's Chemistry Department, seeking admittance into its graduate program. I was told this would necessitate a year of remedial chemistry before I would even be ready to work on my master's degree. Naturally, I was very disappointed, because I could not afford to take that much time.

As I was walking dejectedly across campus, I met an old friend, Leonard Sain, who was then teaching at Wayne State. He asked how I was doing and when I told him, he suggested I talk to Dr. Billig, who was the supervisor for elementary school science education in the School of Education. Sain thought she would be able to help me because of my strong science background. With nothing to lose, and feeling the need to grasp at any straw, I rushed off to see her.

Dr. Billig looked at my record and said, "Mr. Jefferson, with your background in science, after a year of science education courses, I can assure you of a teaching position." This made sense to me, so I earned my teaching certificate at Wayne State and began teaching elementary science at Duffield Elementary School in the fall of 1948. I have no regrets about my decision to enter the field of education because, for the most part, my career in the Detroit Public Schools was both enjoyable and rewarding.

I took classes during the day and worked for the U.S. Special Delivery Mail Service from 4:00 p.m. until 10:00 p.m. Monday through Friday and ten hours on Saturday. I delivered all kinds of things, but I especially remember something called State Sample "Dunners." State Sample was a furniture store on the corner of Michigan and State in downtown Detroit. These "Dunners," which looked like a legal summons, warned that the recipient's wages were going to be garnished if payment for furniture was not forthcoming. This job got me through Wayne State University and put food on the table. I even kept it for a while after I began teaching.

I drove the area that would become zip code 48207. It covered roughly East Warren Avenue to the Detroit River and Woodward Avenue to East Grand Boulevard. This was "Black Bottom," and white drivers refused to drive through it after dark, but for me it was like manna from heaven. I can still see myself, eleven o'clock at night, banging on the side of a rickety house with a flashlight, hollering, "Special Delivery! Special Delivery!" A door would cautiously open and a voice would call out, "Who you want?" I would say, "Special Delivery for so and so." The door would then swing open, the light and warmth of the room would engulf me, and the person would say, "Mailman, come on in and have a piece of chicken. How 'bout a beer?"

Adella and I had moved in with my parents on 28th Street, with the understanding that I would renovate the upstairs three rooms and stay there until we could accumulate enough money to buy our own home. It took me three months to put in new plasterboard walls, electrical circuits, windows, doors, toilet, shower, hot water tank, and an oil stove.

We didn't have two nickels to rub together, but Cohen and Melissa White, Bill and Julia Thomas, Maurice and Marge Letman, Mattie and Dennis Randolph, and all our kids would get together, and we did have fun. We would carry pillows to sit on, and blankets for our kids, because nobody had furniture. We were all in our late twenties, and we had some wild parties.

I taught during the day and drove special delivery at night, and Adella worked in an apron factory on 12th Street, four or five blocks south of Warren Avenue. We saved our money, and by the time our daughter Alexis Louise was born on June 7, 1949, we had accumulated more than $5,000. Now we needed a home more than ever, but there were a couple of problems: We discovered that it was almost impossible to get a mortgage, and there were few places in metropolitan Detroit where blacks could build a new house or even find one to buy. At that time, building a home in Southfield or Birmingham was a death wish for a black family. On the west side of Detroit, no black lived south of Warren Avenue, north of Tireman, or east of Epworth. Blacks also did not live north of Belmont or Trowbridge and very few lived west of Woodward Avenue. Blacks were pretty much restricted to a corridor east of Woodward and south of Gratiot out to East Grand Boulevard.

No white contractor was willing to consider us, even though we had our $5,000 down payment, until I found a German contractor by the name of Theodore L. DeGenhardt, who had begun building houses for blacks in the Conant Garden area. During the war, when the government built the nearby Sojourner Truth Project, whites had rioted to stop blacks from moving in, but now things

The Jefferson home in Grixdale Park.

were slowly beginning to open up. Conant Gardens consisted of about thirty square blocks isolated in northeastern Detroit, just south of 7 Mile Road and bordered on the east by Conant Street, the south by Nevada Street, and the west by Ryan Road. Just to the west of Conant Gardens the small neighborhood of Grixdale Park was also opening up, and we were able to purchase two lots for $1,800. At the time, whites still inhabited this neighborhood of small aluminum-siding homes, interspersed with many vacant lots, but they began moving out when blacks moved in. We hired DeGenhardt to build our home and were then able to secure an FHA mortgage for $8,200 through the United Savings Bank of Detroit. We moved into our new home on June 15, 1951, and I'm still living in the same house.

Along with Harry and Viola Arnold, Leonard and Mae Godbee, and Edsel and Betty Stallings, we organized the Grixdale Park Property Owners Association. We were all young, energetic, and eager to beautify our new homes. I served as president for the first three years. Over the years, I also served in many other positions, and, to this day, I remain the association's agent, which the state of Michigan requires for all 501c-3 nonprofit organizations.

In 1951 we joined Rev. N. H. Holloway's Mitchell Memorial Methodist Church, today known as the Conant Avenue United Methodist Church. Over these past fifty-three years, I have served my church on local, state, and national levels. I have been dean of an interracial camp at Judson Collins Camp and a delegate to the unification of the Methodist Church and the Evangelical United Brethren, which became the United Methodist Church in 1968. I served ten years as youth counselor, seven years as youth choir director, and also as senior choir director, auditor, lay leader, trustee, and historian.

If you were a black teacher in Detroit in 1948, you taught at Duffield, Bishop, Miller, or Sampson. However, as the black population exploded, so too did the teaching assignments. I went to Pattengill Elementary School in 1954 and taught science there until 1969. The principal was Mary Alexander, who ruled the school with an iron fist. She had the distinction of being called "one of the seven devils," because she was one of seven white female principals who served as virtual dictators at their respective schools. She yelled at one and all, even the mailman if he didn't wipe his feet.

I received my master's degree in education in 1954 and then completed thirty hours past the master's in 1960. I was promoted to assistant principal in 1969, although at the time I opposed this assignment. I had passed the written exam four times for assistant principal, each time with a mark of better than 95 percent, but when it came time for the oral interview, I received only 40 percent. I was never given a reason why I failed these oral interviews, but I assumed it was because I appeared too aggressive and confrontational. Then, in 1970, central administration needed an African American administrator to quiet down a militant black school where the parents were dissatisfied with the white administration. I resisted transfer to Halley Elementary School for three weeks, until the administration convinced me that this was a real promotion and that my salary would increase by $3,000.

At the end of my first year at Halley, the principal, Gabriel Venticinque, was transferred to a small elementary school on the far west side, and Bernard Dent, who was black, became the new principal. This meant I had to leave because of an ironic new ruling that now required an integrated staff. I ended up at Ferry Elementary School, from which I retired as assistant principal in 1979.

One of my proudest postwar accomplishments was helping establish the Detroit chapter and later the national organization of Tuskegee Airmen. Ario Dixione, Richard Macon, Henry Peoples, Charley Hill, Wardell Polk, and some other Tuskegee Airmen had proposed an organizational meeting in Detroit. The question was where to hold it. My wife had died in 1970, so they said to me, "Jeff you're single, how about having the meeting at your place?" On July 12, 1972, we held the first organizational meeting of the Detroit Chapter of the Tuskegee Airmen in my home. That same year we organized and hosted our first convention at the Tuller Hotel in downtown Detroit.

The Detroit chapter proved so successful that we helped organize similar chapters in Washington, D.C. and Philadelphia. The Tuskegee Airmen became incorporated in 1975, and we currently have more than thirty chapters, including chapters in Japan, Korea, Germany, England, and Alaska. We have several chapters on Air Force bases for young, active duty personnel. Anyone may join, including civilians, because our objective is "to inspire young people in their educational and professional goals and to succeed in the fields of aviation and aerospace." We want others to learn our history and to spread our heritage. The officers and directors of the organization take no salaries or fees.

Alexander Jefferson and Lillian Eustace.

We preach education and ambition, especially to minority young people. We want them to become aware of the world of space technology and what it takes to live in it. Each year our National Scholarship Fund, which now totals more than $1,700,000, awards at least forty $1,500 grants to deserving disadvantaged high school students. Applicants must have at least a three-point grade average on a four-point scale and be dedicated to a career in aviation, aeronautics, or aerospace. We tell them, "If you would like to go to a college or university or to the Air Force Academy, we'll provide counseling and guidance." In short, we want to do everything we can to help and inspire young people to become productive and fulfilled adults."

I was elected president of the Detroit chapter of the Tuskegee Airmen in 1974 and served as convention host president the following year, when we brought General Chappie James in by helicopter onto the roof of Coho Hall. We had six black generals in attendance, but we couldn't get a single mainstream Detroit newspaper to give us coverage. I wonder why.

Over the years I have also been active in the Tuskegee Airmen Speakers Bureau, which is headquartered in the Tuskegee Airmen National Historical Museum in Detroit's historic Fort Wayne. I speak to schools, churches, youth and senior groups, military organizations, and a wide variety of other audiences. Over the past several years, I have averaged a speech a week.

I am a Life Member of the Silver Falcon Association of the U.S. Air Force Academy and have served since 1978, on a voluntary basis, as an admissions counselor for the Air Force Academy and the Air Force Reserve Officers Training

The first reunion of Tuskegee Airmen was held in Detroit in August 1972. From left to right: Alexander Jefferson, Robert Daniels, Richard Macon, and Robert Oneal. Jefferson, Daniels, and Macon were POWs. Oneal was also shot down but was rescued by the French resistance and returned to base.

Alexander Jefferson and his daughter, Alexis, 1995.

Corps. I am also a Life Member of the American Ex-Prisoner War and a Perpetual Member of the Military Order of the World Wars.

Before she passed away, my wife and I had unofficially adopted a teenager, Ramon Robinson. He eventually became my son. Ramon was once in a swimming pool with a bunch of girls, and he said to one, "My pop should meet your mom." And so, Ramon was responsible for my meeting Lillian Eustace, who became my "significant other." Lillian has not missed a Tuskegee Convention, a P-40 Reunion, the Annual Jazz Cruise, or the Annual Week in Palm Desert since the early 1980s. The first thing my family says when we get together is, "Where's Lillian?" And the first thing her family says is, "Where's Mr. J?" Life is beautiful!

Lt. Col. Alexander Jefferson enshrined in the Michigan Aviation Hall of Fame, October 14, 1995.

On October 14, 1995, I had the great honor of being enshrined in the Michigan Aviation Hall of Fame at the Kalamazoo Aviation Museum in Kalamazoo, Michigan. The Hall was established in 1987 for the purpose of honoring and preserving the history of outstanding Michigan air and space pioneers. Among its members are Roger B. Chafee, Henry Ford, Clarence "Kelly" Johnson, William Powell Lear, Charles A. Lindbergh, Jack R. Lousma, James A. McDivitt, and Brewster H. Shaw Jr. Some of these individuals made aviation their life's work, while others volunteered their time, talent, energies, and insights. All represent the history and spirit of flight, including some who dreamed of its possibilities, others who made it a practical reality, and some who have shown the way to a limitless universe. I was selected for serving this country in one of its finest combat units, The Tuskegee "Red Tails," along with my more than thirty years of dedicated service to the Michigan school system.

I was awarded the Purple Heart on November 9, 2001, authenticated by fellow POW Ewall Ross McCright, who had been directed by the senior American commander to interview every POW entering the South Compound. On October 22, 2004, McCright was posthumously awarded the Legion of Merit—the first American to earn the medal for service as a prisoner of war.

It has been a busy life, and there's no sign that it's slowing down. That's how it should be. I'm happy to have been able to accomplish as much as I have during my lifetime, and to have been a witness to so many positive changes, especially in the area of civil rights. We Americans still face many challenges, but, in my mind, I remain convinced that this is the finest country in the world.

Postscript

The Tuskegee Airmen were dedicated, determined young men who volunteered to become America's first black military airmen. As pioneers, we were determined to serve the United States of America proudly and to the best of our ability, even though many of our fellow citizens, fellow aviators, and commanding officers believed African Americans lacked intelligence, skill, courage, and patriotism.

On the training fields at Tuskegee, we were motivated to excel in everything we did, and that "push to excellence" is as valid today as it was when we were trying to prove to a doubting country that our commitment, skills, and determination matched, and often exceeded, those attributes in our white counterparts in the military. We were, of course, very different individually, but we had in common our sense of discipline, dignity, and accomplishment.

The Tuskegee Airmen, including the ten civilian and military men and women who provided support for each of us pilots, as well as the other one million African Americans who served in World War II, all returned home determined to fight for civil rights for all Americans. We had fought with honor in the skies above and the battlefields below, but we still returned as segregated citizens, forced to continue our battles against bigotry and racism on the home front. White America was quite prepared to ignore the fact that the Tuskegee Airmen had earned 150 Distinguished Flying Crosses, one Legion of Merit, one Silver Star, two Soldier's Medals, fourteen Bronze Stars, eight Purple Hearts, ninety-five Distinguished Flying Crosses, 744 Air Medals, and three Presidential Unit Citations. Sixty-six of our men lost their lives in aerial combat, and even more were killed in training accidents. Another thirty-two of us became prisoners of war.

The Tuskegee Airmen would certainly have received many more prestigious medals if not for the color of our skin. The military's reluctance to award its highest commendations in World Wars I and II to African Americans is well known. After all, to have done so would have been an admission that past segregationist policies had been based on false assumptions. For example, no African American received the Medal of Honor in either World War I or II until 1997, when seven World War II black servicemen were belatedly honored. Only one of them was alive to accept his medal.

As an African American, I had, of course, experienced discrimination throughout my life. Often it was covert, but it could also be overt. In graduate school, I had a history professor who literally called me a liar when I wrote a term paper on my experiences as a World War II fighter pilot. He told me that Negroes did not have the intelligence to enter the Air Force and that I had fabricated my story. He also did not believe a Negro could earn an "A" in his class, because we supposedly were incapable of such high-quality work. I proved him wrong, but only after I went to the dean with my term paper along with the results of the tests I had taken in class.

The postwar civil rights movement was just beginning when I returned from service, but it profoundly affected my personal and professional life. It convinced me that so many things I had only dreamed of as a youth could now be part of my reality. As Tuskegee Airmen, we knew we had served our country with distinction in battle, but now we also wanted to join the civil rights movement and do everything we could to break down the remaining racial barriers within both the military and civilian sectors.

Today discrimination tends to be more subtle, and it is often institutional. It is harder to discern when whites, usually male, get together in private clubs and businesses, in political and legal chambers, and even in institutions of higher learning to determine policies. Such decisions, of course, affect the well-being of all Americans, but especially African Americans, who historically have been absent from the seats of power. Nevertheless, our young people need to move beyond racism, just as we were forced to do when we were determined to fly. After all, if you are able to succeed in spite of the barriers erected by individuals and institutions, you emerge a much stronger human being.

Because we had clearly proven ourselves as airmen, we were confident we could make the country we fought and died for a better place for all Americans. General Daniel "Chappie" James, who was one of the 992 Tuskegee pilots and who would later become the Air Force's first African American four-star general, said it best for all of us: "This is my country: I will hold her hand. I will fight for her. I shall protect her, but I'll make her treat me the way she should."

Coleman Young, the late mayor of Detroit and a Tuskegee Airman navigator in the 477th Bombardment Group, also emphasized our determination: "We learned how to survive in the air, and when we hit the ground, while white pilots rested, we continued our struggle to preserve our dignity as human beings. All of us are better and stronger for the experience."

Mayor Young was referring to the Double V campaign waged by all World War II African American servicemen and servicewomen. Simply put, we had to fight for victory on two fronts: first, against the racism of the Axis powers, and then against the segregation and discrimination of our own country.

Times have changed, and the social, economic, and, indeed, human compromises we too often had been forced to make were no longer tenable in postwar America. Inclusion was the benchmark, and we took our first great postwar step on July 26, 1948, when President Harry S. Truman issued Executive Order 9981 calling for the desegregation of the Armed Forces. Without question, his decision was certainly made easier because of the wartime achievements of the Tuskegee Airmen. Next came the Supreme Court's 1954 *Brown v. Board of Education* school desegregation decision, followed by the Civil Rights Acts of 1964, 1965, and 1968, all of which brought us closer to the ideal, expressed so well in 1776 by Thomas Jefferson and other signers of the Declaration of Independence that "all men are created equal [and] endowed by their creator with certain inalienable rights."

The social and legal changes of the postwar era also brought the Tuskegee Airmen the kind of official and popular recognition they had long deserved. There are now more than fifteen books about the Tuskegee Airmen, at least three documentaries, and one Hollywood feature film. We also have a special exhibit in the United State Air Force Museum at Wright-Patterson Air Force Base, just outside of Dayton, Ohio, as well as our own Tuskegee Airmen National Museum in Detroit.

Looking back, what did it all mean? Tuskegee Airman Ed Gleed said it so well for all of us: "When we were in training at Tuskegee and in combat, we never gave it a thought that we were making history. All we wanted was to learn to fly as Army Air Corps pilots, fight for our country, and survive."

Some sixty years have passed since we flew the unfriendly skies over Nazi Germany, but we Tuskegee Airmen are still fighter pilots. We have our reunions and we reminisce and laugh about "the good old days." But we also are very proud of the changes we helped bring about both within and outside the military. Above all, we want our fellow Americans to know that the civil rights we fought so hard for are not for African Americans alone, but for all human beings.

In the final analysis, the Tuskegee Airmen did make history, and I am so very proud to have been one of them.

Appendix

Alexander Jefferson's Organizational Affiliations

Air Force Association

American Ex-Prisoner of War Association of the United States

Clark-Atlanta University Alumni Association

Conant Avenue United Methodist Church: Chairman, Trustees Committee

Detroit Organization of School Administrators and Supervisors

Ethnic Minority Higher Education Task Force, United Methodist Church

Howard University Alumni Association

Metropolitan Detroit Science Administrators

Michigan Association of Supervision and Curriculum Study

Michigan Retired Officers Association

Military Order of the World Wars

National Officers Association

P-40 Warhawk Pilot Association

P-51 Mustang Association

Reserve Officers Association of the United States

The Retired Officers Association

Tuskegee Airmen, Inc.

Wayne State University Alumni

Yankee Air Force

Alexander Jefferson's Military Awards

Air Force Achievement Medal

Air Force Longevity Service Medal

Air Medal

American Campaign Medal

American Defense Service Medal

Armed Forces Reserve Medal

European-African-Middle Eastern Campaign Medal

National Defense Service Medal

Prisoner of War Medal

Purple Heart

World War II Victory Medal

Selected Sources

Books

Beltrone, Art, and Lee Beltrone. *A Wartime Log*. Charlottesville, VA: Howell, 1995.

Bennett, Lerone. *Before the Mayflower: A History of Black America, 1619–1962*. Chicago: Johnson, 1969, 2000.

Bowers, William T., et al. *Black Soldier White Army*. Washington, DC: U.S. Government Printing Office, 1996.

Carlson, Lewis H. *We Were Each Other's Prisoners: An Oral History of World War II American and German Prisoners of War*. New York: Basic Books, 1997.

Dalfiume, Richard M. *Fighting on Two Fronts: Desegregation of the U.S. Armed Forces, 1939–1953*. Columbia: University of Missouri Press, 1969.

Daniel, Eugene L. *In the Presence of Mine Enemies: An American Chaplain in World War II German Prison Camps*. Attleboro, MA: self-published, 1985.

Davis, Benjamin O., Jr. *Benjamin O. Davis, Jr., American: An Autobiography*. Washington, DC: Smithsonian Institution Press, 1991.

Davis, Lenwood G., and George Hill. *Blacks in the American Armed Forces, 1776–1983: A Bibliography*. Westport, CT: Greenwood Press, 1985.

Dryden, Charles W. *A-Train: Memoirs of a Tuskegee Airman*. Tuscaloosa: University of Alabama Press, 1997.

Durand, Arthur. *Stalag Luft III: The Secret Story*. Baton Rouge: Louisiana State University Press, 1988.

Francis, Charles E., and Adolph Caso. *The Tuskegee Airmen: The Men Who Changed a Nation*. Boston: Branden, 1997.

———. *Tuskegee Airmen: The Story of the Negro in the U.S. Air Force*. Boston: Branden, 1993.

Franklin, John Hope. *From Slavery to Freedom: A History of Negro Americans*. New York: Knopf, 1947; repr. 1997.

George, Linda, and George Charles. *The Tuskegee Airmen*. Portsmouth, NH: Arcadia Tempus, 1998.

Greene, Robert Ewell. *A Pictorial Tribute to the Tuskegee Airmen*. Self-published, n.d.

Gropman, Alan L. *The Air Force Integrates, 1945–1964*. Washington, DC: U.S. Government Printing Office, 1978.

Gupert, Betty Kaplan. *Invisible Wings: An Annotated Bibliography on Blacks in Aviation, 1916–1993*. Westport, CT: Greenwood Press, 1994.

Hardesty, Von, and Dominick Pisano. *Black Wings: The American Black in Aviation*. Washington, DC: Smithsonian Institution Press, 1984.

Homan, Lynn M., and Thomas Reilly. *Black Knights: The Story of the Tuskegee Airmen*. Gretna, LA: Pelican, 2001.

Homan, Lynn M., et al. *Tuskegee Airmen: American Heroes*. Gretna, LA: Pelican, 2002.

Jakeman, Robert J. *The Divided Skies: The Establishing Segregated Flight Training at Tuskegee, Alabama, 1934–1942*. Tuscaloosa: University of Alabama Press, 1992.

Kimball, R. W. *Clipped Wings*. Dayton, OH: R. W. Kimball, 1948; repr., Baltimore: Gateway, 1992.

King, Desmond. *Separate and Unequal: Black Americans and the U.S. Federal Government*. New York: Oxford University Press, 1997.

Lanning, Michael Lee. *The African-American Soldier: From Crispus Attucks to Colin Powell*. Secaucus, NJ: Birch Lane Press, 1997.

Lee, Ulysses. *The Employment of the Negro Troops*. Washington, DC: U.S. Government Printing Office, 1966.

MacGregor, Morris J. *Integration of the Armed Forces, 1940–1965*. Washington, DC: U.S. Government Printing Office, 1981.

McGovern, James R. *Black Eagle: General Daniel "Chappie" James, Jr.* Tuscaloosa: University of Alabama Press, 1985.

McKee, Daniel C. *50 Years Later: Stalag Luft III Diary*. N. Richland Hills, TX: Smithfield Press, 1999.

McKissack, Patricia, et al. *Red-Tail Angels: The Story of the Tuskegee Airmen in World War II*. New York: Walker & Co., 2001.

Motley, Mary Penick, ed. *The Invisible Soldier: The Experiences of the Black Soldier, World War II*. Detroit: Wayne State University Press, 1975.

Neary, Bob. *Stalag Luft III: Sagan . . . Nuremberg . . . Moosburg: A Collection of German Prison Camp Sketches with Descriptive Text Based on Personal Experiences*. North Wales, PA: self-published, 1946; repr., Eighth Air Force Association, 1992.

Nichols, Lee. *Breakthrough on the Color Front*. Pueblo, CO: Passeggiata Press, 1993.

Osur, Alan M. *Blacks in the Army Air Forces During World War II: The Problem of Race Relations*. Washington, DC: U.S. Government Printing Office, 1977.

Phelps, J. Alfred. *Chappie: America's First Black Four-Star General: The Life and Times of Daniel James, Jr.* Novato, CA: Presidio Press, 1991.

Rollins, Charles. *Stalag Luft III: The Full Story*. New York: Hyperion Books, 1992.

Rose, Robert A. *Lonely Eagles: The Story of America's Black Air Force in World War II*. Los Angeles: Tuskegee Airmen, Los Angeles Chapter, 1976.

Sandler, Stanley. *Segregated Skies: All-Black Combat Squadrons of WW II*. Washington, DC: Smithsonian Institution Press, 1992.

Scott, Lawrence P., and William M. Womack. *Double V: The Civil Rights Struggle of the Tuskegee Airmen*. East Lansing: Michigan State University Press, 1994.

Silvera, John D. *The Negro in World War II*. Manchester, NH: Ayer, 1974.

Smith, Charlene E. McGee, et al. *Tuskegee Airman: The Biography of Charles E. McGee, Air Force Fighter Combat Record Holder*. Boston: Branden, 1999.

Spivey, Delmar. *POW Odyssey: Recollections of Center Compound, Stalag Luft III and the Secret German Peace Mission in World War II*. Attleboro, MA: Colonial Lithograph, 1984.

Takaki, Ronald T. *Double Victory: A Multicultural History of America in World War II*. Boston: Little, Brown, 2000.

Toliver, Raymond F. *The Interrogator: The Story of Hanns Joachim Scharff, Master Interrogator of the Luftwaffe*. Atglen, PA: Schiffer Military History, 1997.

Warren, James C. *The Tuskegee Airmen Mutiny at Freeman Field*. San Rafael, CA: Conyers, 1998.

White, Walter. *A Rising Wind. A Report on the Negro Soldier in the European Theatre of War*. Westport, CT: Greenwood, 1978.

———. *A Man Called White: The Autobiography of Walter White*. New York: Viking Press, 1948.

Wright, Arnold A. *Behind the Wire: Stalag Luft III, South Compound*. Benton, Arkansas: self-published, 1993.

Wynne, Neil A. *The Afro-American and the Second World War*. NY: Holmes and Meier, 1975.

Young, Coleman. *Hard Stuff: The Autobiography of Coleman Young*. NY: Viking Press, 1994.

Articles

"Air Force Ethics Once a Black, White Matter." *The State News* (Lansing, MI), May 13, 1983.

Baird, Woody. "Tuskegee Airmen Underscore Point They're Americans." *Huntsville Times*, August 19, 2001.

Boettcher, Thomas D. "Smithsonian Saluting Black Pilots." *Christian Science Monitor*, n.d.

Brooks, T. "Tuskegee Airmen Make Black History Come Alive." *Michigan Chronicle*, January 23–29, 2001.

Buck, Sue. "Former Tuskegee Airman Shares His Story at Cloverdale." *Farmington Observer*, January 17, 2002.

Cummings, Marc A. "The Tuskegee Airmen: Greatness in Our Midst." *Michigan Chronicle*, February 6, 2001.

Cole, James L. "Dulag Luft Recalled and Revisited." *Aerospace Historian* XIX (June 1972).

Friedheim, Eric. "Welcome to Dulag Luft." *Air Force* XXVIII (September 1945).

Gavrilovich, Peter. "Air Force Removes Racial Reprimand from Black Aviators' WWII Record." *Detroit Free Press*, August 26, 1995.

———. "Tuskegee Airmen Helped U.S. Make Giant Leap," *Detroit Free Press*, July 18, 1989.

"The Genesis and Growth of the National Organization of Tuskegee Airmen, Inc." *Molding a Black Legacy*. Tuskegee Airmen, Inc., 1989.

Goldstein, Richard. "Gen. Benjamin O. Davis Jr, 89, Dies; Dispelled Racial Myths as Leader of Pilots' Unit." *New York Times*, July 7, 2002.

Gropman, Alan. "Why the Services Are Integrated." *Air Force Times*, February 26, 1996.

Hennessy, Tom. "Race Never Grounded Ex-Pilot." *Long Beach Press-Telegram*, April 10, 2001.

Jackson, Irvin L. "Colonel Urges NAACP Crowd to Remember." *Port Huron Times Herald*, October 28, 1995.

Jefferson, Alexander. "Life as a Black POW." *Tony Brown's Journal* (March 1983).

Jefferson, Alexander, and Barbara Hoover. "North or South, He Was Hardened to Racism." *Detroit News*, February 16, 1990.

Kwan, Joshua L. "Tuskegee Airman Inspires Kids to Soar on Their Dreams." *San Jose Mercury News*, December 13, 2001.

Mackay, Katurah. "The Redtail Angels." *National Parks Magazine* (January/February 1999).

McClellan, Theresa D. "Air Legends: First Black Fighter Pilots Give Students Firsthand History Lesson." *Grand Rapids Press*, March 26, 2002.

McCollum, Berkley. "America's Forgotten Eagles." *Aviation Quarterly* 7, no. 2 (1983).

Moore, Lynn. "High Fliers: Airmen Describe Aerial Feats at Rocketry Event." *Muskegon Chronicle*, April 26, 2003.

"More Charges Leveled Against Selfridge Field." *Michigan Chronicle*, February 26, 1944.

Mullen, Frank. "Black Pilots' Past and Future Keep Stress on Excellence." *Denver Post*, August 7, 1981.

Palmer, Ken. "WW II Pilot Offers Words of Hope." *Flint Journal*, May 4, 2001.

Percy, William Alexander. "Jim Crow and Uncle Sam: The Tuskegee Flying Units and the U.S. Army Air Forces in Europe During World War II." *Journal of Military History* (July 2003).

Perry, Mylinda. "Pilot Helps Experiment, Air Force Integrated." *State News*, May 16, 1983.

Plammer, Philip, ed., "Dulag Luft." *Aerospace Historian* XIX (June 1972).

Rosencrantz, Rene A. "WW II Pilot Brings History to Life." *Clio Register*, January 26, 2003.

Scharff, Hans Joachim. "Without Torture." *Argosy* (May 1950).

"Selfridge Field Rumor Denied by War Department." *Michigan Chronicle*, May 13, 1944.

Strebe, Amy Goodpaster. "Red-Tailed Angel." *Mountain View Voice*, December 21, 2001.

"Tuskegee Airman Proud to Serve." *The Tennessean*, August 19, 2001.

"Tuskegee Airmen: Removal of Reprimands Was Long Overdue." *Detroit Free Press*, August 29, 1995.

Williams, Teresa Taylor. "Famous Airmen Reach Heights." *Muskegon Chronicle*, May 9, 1988.

Dissertations and Theses

Bland, Edwin A., Jr. "German Methods for Interrogation of Captured Allied Aircrews." M.A. thesis, Air Command and Staff School of Air University, Maxwell Air Force Base, 1948.

Burbank, Lyman B. "A History of the American Air Force Prisoners of War in Center Compound, Stalag Luft III, Germany." M.A. thesis, University of Chicago, 1946.

Goldman, Ben. "German Treatment of American Prisoners of War in World War II." M.A. thesis, Wayne State University, 1949.

Hasselbring, Andrew S. "American Prisoners of War in the Third Reich." Ph.D. dissertation, Temple University, 1991.

Films

Nightfighters: The True Story of the 332nd Fighter Group—The Tuskegee Airmen. Xenon Studios, 1994.

The Negro Soldier. U.S. Army, 1944.

The Tuskegee Airmen. HBO, 1995.

The Tuskegee Airmen. Rubicon Productions, 2003.

The Tuskegee Airmen: American Heroes. Goldhill Home Media, 1998.

Museums

Tuskegee Airmen National Museum, 6325 West Jefferson Ave., Detroit, MI 48209.

United States Air Force Museum, Wright-Patterson Air Force Base, Dayton, OH 45433.

Internet Sites and Publications

"Afro-Americans and the Military, 1939 to 1945." www.lib.umich.edu/libhome/Documents.center/blackww2.html.

Brandon, MSgt. Linda E. "Black Pilots Shatter Myths." http://ac.acusd.edu/History/WW2Timeline/HOYT/shatter.html.

Brown, Avonie, and Brian Klaas. "The Tuskegee Airmen." www.afroam.org/history/tusk/tuskmain.html.

"A Chronology of African American Military Service From WWI Through WWII." www.redstone.army.mil/history/integrate/chron3b.htm.

Conyers Publishing Company. "Hero of the Month." www.tuskegee.com/heroof.htm.

The History Place. "African-Americans in World War II." www.historyplace.com/unitedstates/aframerwar.

Hoyt, Davina. "Tuskegee Airmen of World War II." http://ac.acusd.edu/History/WW2Timeline/Tuskegee.html.

"Integration of the Air Force." www.afroam.org/history/tusk/integrate.html.

Lowe, Merrie Schilter. "Letters of Reprimand Removed from Tuskegee Airmen's Records." http://ac.acusd.edu/History/WW2Timeline/HOYT/removed.html.

McRae, Bennie J. "Tuskegee Airmen: Lest We Forget." www.coax.net/people/lwf/tus_air.html.

"Meet Lt. Colonel Alexander Jefferson." www.quest.nasa.gov/people/bios/aero/jeffersona.html.

Smith, Col. William J. "The Tuskegee Airmen." www.achiever.com/freehmpg/tai.

"The Tuskegee Airman Mutiny." www.tuskegee.com/index.html.

"Tuskegee Airman Shares Experiences." www.aetc.randolph.af.mil/pa/AETCNS/Mar2000/00–075.htm.

"Tuskegee Airmen, Inc." www.tuskegeeairmen.org.

"Tuskegee Airmen of World War II." http://ac.acusd.edu/History/WW2Timeline/Tuskegee.html.

Other Sources

Russell, Kim. *Tuskegee Love Letters: Letters written by James B. Knighten and His Wife: A One-Act Play.* 702 Entertainment and Productions, n.d.

Tuskegee Airmen Trading Card Collector Sets. Long Beach, CA: Mint Cards, n.d.

Index

Note: Page numbers followed by "f" indicate an illustration.

World War II The Global, Human, and Ethical Dimension

G . KURT PIEHLER, series editor

DATE DUE

DEC 28 2005		
JAN 2 5 2006		
APR 2 5 2006		
JUL 2 5 2007		

GAYLORD   #3523PI   Printed in USA